COMBAT AIRCRAFT

149 Bf 109 *JABO* UNITS IN THE WEST

SERIES EDITOR TONY HOLMES

149

COMBAT AIRCRAFT

Malcolm V Lowe

Bf 109 *JABO* UNITS IN THE WEST

OSPREY
PUBLISHING

OSPREY PUBLISHING
Bloomsbury Publishing Plc
Kemp House, Chawley Park, Cumnor Hill, Oxford, OX2 9PH, UK
29 Earlsfort Terrace, Dublin 2, Ireland
1385 Broadway, 5th Floor, New York, NY 10018, USA
E-mail: info@ospreypublishing.com
www.ospreypublishing.com

OSPREY is a trademark of Osprey Publishing Ltd

First published in Great Britain in 2023

A catalogue record for this book is available from the British Library.

ISBN: PB 9781472854452; eBook 9781472854469; ePDF 9781472854445;
XML 9781472854438

23 24 25 26 27   10 9 8 7 6 5 4 3 2 1

Edited by Tony Holmes
Cover Artwork by Gareth Hector
Aircraft Profiles by Jim Laurier
Index by Alan Rutter
Typeset by PDQ Digital Media Solutions, UK
Printed and bound in India by Replika Press Private Ltd

Osprey Publishing supports the Woodland Trust, the UK's leading woodland
conservation charity.

To find out more about our authors and books visit **www.ospreypublishing.com**.
Here you will find extracts, author interviews, details of forthcoming events and
the option to sign up for our newsletter.

Acknowledgements
The Author gratefully acknowledges help and advice from historian friends and
researchers, including Eddie J Creek, Robert Forsyth, Chris Goss, Marc-André
Haldimann, Histor Center AB Brustem, Hans Meier, John Levesley, Jeff
Litchfield, Georg Morrison, Robin Powell, Andy Saunders, Hendrik
Schoebrechts, Jim Smith, Andy Sweet, Peter Walter, John Weal and Graham
Young. Particular thanks to Floyd Blair, P-47D Thunderbolt pilot with the 404th
Fighter Group (FG) of the Ninth Air Force, who successfully passed the
101-years-old milestone still with vivid memories of the events of 1 January 1945.
Finally, a special mention for the late John Batchelor MBE, whose many years of
research into the Luftwaffe and meetings with its former personnel were a part of
the background for this book.

Front Cover
One of the most successful exponents of
the *Jabo* Bf 109 was Oberleutnant (later
Hauptmann) Frank Liesendahl. An
accomplished enthusiast for fighter-bomber
operations, he developed the *Liesendahl
Verfahren* ('Liesendahl Method') for
attacking ground targets and shipping.
As the *Staffelkapitän* of 13./JG 2 (later
re-designated as 10./JG 2), he led by
example and carried out a series of
damaging *Jabo* raids with his fellow pilots
that the British defences found difficult
to counter.

One of the prime targets for Liesendahl
and his unit was merchant shipping in
coastal convoys sailing along the English
Channel coast. Liesendahl's method of
attack involved approaching the intended
victim at wave-top height, followed by a fast
climb and a brief shallow dive towards the
target, during which the underfuselage
250-kg bomb was lobbed at the ship in a
rapid pull-up. In this way Liesendahl's unit
achieved a number of successes against
coastal shipping, as well as striking at a
variety of ground targets including the
Telecommunications Research
Establishment west of Worth Matravers
in Dorset.

In this specially commissioned artwork,
Gareth Hector has depicted Liesendahl
flying his well-known Bf 109F-4/B
Wk-Nr 7629 'Blue 1' while making one
of his characteristic attacks on a merchant
ship off the Channel coast of southern
England.

PREVIOUS PAGES
The most famous example of the 'Friedrich'
Jabo was Bf 109F-4/B Wk-Nr 7629 'Blue
1' (also depicted in the cover artwork),
flown by Oberleutnant Frank Liesendahl,
Staffelkapitän of 13.(*Jabo*)/JG 2, from
Beaumont-le-Roger in the early spring
of 1942 – this photograph of the aircraft,
with Liesendahl in the cockpit, was taken
on 31 March. Although this unit was
eventually re-designated 10.(*Jabo*)/JG 2,
it retained the blue numbering of the 13.
Staffel and the unique unit markings of a
blue chevron and bar behind the fuselage
cross. 'Blue 1's' rudder featured an
impressive scoreboard of anti-shipping
successes credited to Liesendahl and his
pilots (*Tony Holmes Collection*)

CONTENTS

CHAPTER ONE

IN THE BEGINNING

It has often proven to be the case that wartime necessity brings about rapid change and innovation. This can certainly be said for the rise of the high-performance fighter-bomber. World War 2 witnessed the development and eventually widespread employment of this specialist and specially equipped type of aircraft, often but not exclusively using existing airframes suitably adapted. The first innovators in the creation of a modern, capable and well-equipped fighter-bomber force were the Germans. For a comparatively short time during World War 2, the Luftwaffe was effectively the exclusive user of this new but potentially deadly type of aircraft. In German, the term 'fighter-bomber' is translated as *Jagdbomber*, abbreviated simply to *Jabo*.

The *Jabo*, as a major frontline type of aircraft for the Luftwaffe, grew out of a series of circumstances, not least of these being pragmatism when faced with operational realities that needed to be adapted to. Indeed, the *Jabo* developed from several largely unrelated operational profiles and requirements that nevertheless came together during 1940 to make the Messerschmitt Bf 109 into the first major fighter-bomber of its generation.

It was singularly appropriate that this accolade was applied to the Bf 109. One of the greatest fighters of all time, the type played a pivotal role for the Luftwaffe during World War 2. Indeed, many considered it to be, at the height of its operational prowess, the best fighter in the world. The famous Luftwaffe fighter ace Adolf Galland was in no doubt as to the usefulness

The He 51 was the Luftwaffe's principal fighter when the Spanish Civil War began in 1936. When its shortcomings against modern combat aircraft were exposed, the type found a new niche performing air-to-ground operations, paving the way for the development and refinement of this method of warfare in the following years. This He 51B or C of J/88 was photographed in Spain, illustrating markings adopted there for the Nationalist forces and their German allies (*Malcolm V Lowe Collection*) of the Bf 109 during the opening months of World War 2. Interviewed by the RAF's Air Historical Branch in 1953, he explained, 'The Me 109 gave us a tool to take on and defeat the enemy ranged against us'. He further pointed out, 'The Me 109 not only possessed superior features, but it also caused a revolution in fighter design throughout the world'.

Prior to World War 2, the fighter-bomber as an operational concept had been developing as a part of Luftwaffe strategy, albeit from small but important beginnings. The Spanish Civil War commenced during the summer of 1936, started by Spanish Nationalist rebels led by Gen Francisco Franco who began an uprising against the legitimate Spanish (Republican) government. With the onset of this conflict, Nazi Germany provided considerable military assistance to the Nationalists. Part of this aid constituted frontline aviation assets organised as the *Legion Condor*, which was established in November 1936 under the command of Generalmajor Hugo Sperrle, with Oberstleutnant Wolfram Freiherr von Richthofen as its chief-of-staff. It was ostensibly made up of Luftwaffe 'volunteers'.

Amongst the first German aircraft shipped to Spain for support of the Nationalists was the Heinkel He 51 biplane fighter. At that time the He 51 was the main German frontline fighter, although a major replacement was on the horizon in the shape of the Bf 109. The He 51 had initially entered Luftwaffe service during 1934. Six He 51s were shipped to Spain in August 1936 as a starting point in the fighter assistance to Gen Franco's Nationalist forces, nominally for use by Spanish pilots.

A substantial amount of aid subsequently flowed from Germany, including a large number of He 51s in several batches. More than 150 examples are eventually thought to have been shipped to Spain. Within the *Legion Condor*, the He 51s were flown by up to four *Staffeln* (squadrons) of the fighter *Jagdgruppe* (group) J/88. A number of pilots who later became well known during World War 2 flew the type in combat over Spain against the air force of the legitimate Spanish government, including Johannes 'Hannes' Trautloft and Adolf Galland.

At first all went well for the German fighters when they encountered outdated and often antiquated Spanish Republican aircraft in aerial combat. However, aid for the Spanish government from the Soviet Union increasingly included more formidable opponents in the form of Polikarpov I-15 biplane fighters and, a little later, the small but powerful I-16 'Rata' monoplane. Aerial combat against these types showed the He 51 to be outclassed, and losses of both Luftwaffe and Spanish Nationalist He 51 pilots increased.

This started to be a serious concern from February 1937 onwards, forcing the *Legion Condor* to revise the operational profile of the He 51 so that the *Staffeln* equipped with the aircraft concentrated more on tactical ground-attack duties, while increasingly assigning fighter tasks to the Bf 109. Examples of the latter arrived in Spain in significant numbers during the first half of 1937. These included early Jumo-engined Bf 109Bs, and eventually the similarly powered Bf 109D also became vitally important to the air war over Spain.

The reassigned He 51s subsequently enjoyed some success against ground targets, the type finding a new role undertaking low-level light bombing and strafing sorties. Thus, acting as a makeshift attack aircraft, the He 51 proved unexpectedly adept in this new role. In that sense it can be regarded as the first 'modern' fighter-bomber, albeit operating principally in a tactical attack configuration close to the frontlines, as had been the case with the earliest fighter-bomber types in the latter stages of World War 1. So important was this role for the He 51 that the third *Staffel* of J/88, 3.J/88, was specifically tasked with flying fighter-bomber sorties upon its formation in December 1936.

Fitted with racks to carry two small bombs under each wing, in addition to its two 7.92 mm machine guns mounted in the upper forward fuselage, the He 51 proved to have a useful offensive capability. It was in this capacity that then-Leutnant Adolf Galland first started to make a name for himself. Tasked with the air-to-ground mission, he 'cut his teeth' on this type of frontline work, although it was not his preferred form of operational flying.

The Heinkels proved to be especially useful during the fighting in the Republican-supporting Basque areas in the north of Spain particularly around Bilbao, although the type generally proved to be effective wherever it was deployed. In some cases the low-flying strafing and bombing Heinkel fighters were able to hit targets that the *Legion Condor*'s twin-engined bombers had found

A neat and very close formation of Luftwaffe He 51s. The Germans saw the propaganda value of such images, which were circulated widely. He 51s saw a considerable amount of combat with the *Legion Condor* during the Spanish Civil War, primarily as makeshift fighter-bombers. Adolf Galland flew the type in Spain, but was never truly at home with air-to-ground operations, preferring aerial combat throughout his frontline career (*Malcolm V Lowe Collection*)

difficult to locate. They were also effective when called upon to operate at short notice if a new target of importance that needed rapidly attacking was discovered during the ground fighting.

The Bf 109 eventually completely replaced the He 51 in the fighter role within the *Legion Condor*'s J/88. Although the Messerschmitts were employed mainly on pure fighter and bomber escort duties until the end of the Spanish Civil War in early 1939, some strafing sorties were indeed flown. This was the Bf 109's baptism of fire in that mission profile, and it was a significant portent of what was to come a short time later.

In the immediate term, however, the success of the He 51s in supporting ground forces was further developed in Spanish skies by the use of the Junkers Ju 87 dive-bomber and, to a lesser extent, the Henschel Hs 123 biplane in the tactical attack role. Both types proved effective in Spain, particularly the Ju 87. Both had been designed as dive-bombers, although the Hs 123 proved better suited to flying the type of low-level attack profiles that the He 51 had pioneered.

The use of air power in support of ground forces, either directly over the battlefield or in clearing the way for the army to advance, was of particular interest to Oberstleutnant von Richthofen. He is often credited as being one of the chief developers of this type of tactic during the war in Spain, and afterwards in the early years of World War 2. It became a very important part of the Luftwaffe's mission profiles, and was further refined and developed during the latter conflict.

This line-up of Bf 109E-3s from *Stab J/88* was probably photographed at El Prat de Llobregat, near Barcelona, in March 1939. Only a small number of 'Emils' became operational in Spain before the civil war ended, although earlier marks of Bf 109 had seen combat with the *Legion Condor* in growing numbers from 1937. The Bf 109 replaced the He 51 in the pure fighter role for J/88, but it was also involved in limited and often impromptu air-to-ground strafing operations as required or when the opportunity arose (*Malcolm V Lowe Collection*)

By the end of the Spanish Civil War, the Bf 109 was established as the Luftwaffe's main frontline fighter. The type had first flown during 1935, and the initial production series of the Messerschmitt up to and including the Bf 109D were powered by the Junkers Jumo 210 inline engine. From the Bf 109E onwards, the engine of choice was the more powerful Daimler-Benz DB 601 in a much more streamlined airframe arrangement. The Bf 109E had began reaching operational Luftwaffe *Jagdgeschwader* (JG – fighter wings) in early 1939, but by the start of World War 2, on 1 September 1939, the 'Emil' had not fully replaced the Bf 109C/D in all frontline Luftwaffe fighter units. The two differently powered types therefore fought together in the skies over Poland during the first weeks of the war.

The 'Emil' was a major advance over the Jumo-engined Bf 109 that had preceded it, being more streamlined and powerful. It was this variant that was to be diverted from being simply a fighter into the developing and specialised role of fighter-bomber.

The initial production model of the 'Emil' series was the Bf 109E-1, which was powered by the DB 601A inline engine, nominally of 1100 hp (note that German calculations for 'horsepower' are slightly different to the similar imperial reading). This was some 300 hp more than was available from the Jumo 210 engine of the Bf 109D, but conversely the Daimler-Benz unit was around 400 lbs heavier. In terms of armament, the Bf 109E-1 inherited the arrangement established for the Jumo-engined Bf 109s of two MG 17 7.92 mm machine guns mounted in the upper forward fuselage ahead of the cockpit above the rear part of the engine bay. A similar machine gun was mounted in each wing. The E-1 was the principal Bf 109 mark of the first months of World War 2.

However, the next major production model, the Bf 109E-3, introduced a much heavier armament. Although the two MG 17 machine guns in the upper forward fuselage were retained for the E-3, the wing-mounted MG 17s were replaced by MG FF 20 mm cannon, one in each wing. This was a much larger and heavier weapon than the MG 17, and it was mounted slightly further outboard than the machine gun – a prominent bulge on the wing undersurface was introduced so that the cannon and its associated 60-round drum magazine could be accommodated within the 'Emil's' wing. The Bf 109 had not been intended to house such a bulky weapon within its mainplanes. Indeed, the Bf 109's wing had not been designed with the carriage of weapons, internal or external, as a primary consideration at all.

At that time the MG FF was already becoming obsolete, and it had a slow rate of fire of some 530 rounds per minute. The cannon did, however, represent a significant up-gunning of the Bf 109. The E-3 also introduced several further improvements over the E-1. During production of the Bf 109E-3 series a new, square-framed cockpit canopy was introduced

that replaced the more rounded shape of previous versions, although some older aircraft had the new canopy retrofitted. This mark of 'Emil' was most prominent during the Battle of France period of the *Blitzkrieg*.

Factory-installed armour plate within the canopy for the pilot's head was included from the Bf 109E-4 onwards. Again, there was some retro-fitting of this important feature in earlier 'Emils'. A development of the MG FF, the MG FF/M which fired a slightly different and potentially more potent type of cannon armament was made available for use in the Bf 109 and was fitted instead of the standard MG FF in later aircraft – notably many of the Bf 109E-4s and subsequent marks of the 'Emil'. It was this type that began supplementing the E-3 in the latter stages of the Battle of France, and was particularly important during the Battle of Britain.

The Bf 109E series was also widely built by several manufacturers in addition to the parent company at Regensburg and Augsburg. They included Erla at Leipzig, Fieseler at Kassel and AGO Flugzeugwerke at Oschersleben. 'Emils' were produced from the second half of 1938 onwards, entering increasingly numerous Luftwaffe service in the first half of 1939 and also serving comparatively briefly in the later stages of the Spanish Civil War. During the *Blitzkrieg* period of the opening months of World War 2, the 'Emil' played a vital role in the Luftwaffe's operations. This included the invasion of Poland, the protracted but ultimately successful attack on Norway and the large-scale offensive against France and the Low Countries starting on 10 May 1940. During this time the Bf 109 operated primarily in its intended role as a dedicated fighter, in which it excelled particularly against inferior or badly organised opposition.

However, similar to the previous operations during the Spanish Civil War, the type was also employed for impromptu air-to-ground missions. This took place particularly when opposing aircraft were absent or had been swept from the skies, allowing the Messerschmitt pilots to seek out ground targets – these sometimes included airfields. A number of Luftwaffe pilots began adding to their aerial victories with ground claims

A Bf 109E of 1./JG 1 has its DB 601 engine fettled behind a gaggle of Hs 123 biplanes at an austere airfield somewhere in northern France during the Battle of France in May 1940. The rugged ground-attack Henschels belonged to II.(S)/LG 2, and this unit later became the principal *Jabo* operator of fighter-bomber Bf 109Es during the Battle of Britain (*Tony Holmes Collection*)

Erla-built Bf 109E-3 Wk-Nr 1361 was a highly important test airframe that was used in the development of the *Jabo* layout for the 'Emil'. Bearing the Stammkennzeichen CA+NK, it is seen here fitted with an underfuselage ETC 500 stores rack (and a 500-kg SD 250 bomb), which became standard for both the Bf 109E and the later Bf 109F *Jabo* fighter-bombers. The ETC 500 was mounted slightly offset to port *(Malcolm V Lowe Collection)*

Bf 109E-3 Wk-Nr 1361 was also used for the successful development of an installation for the 250-kg SC 250 bomb under the centre fuselage. The ETC stores rack turned the 'Emil' into a true fighter-bomber *(Malcolm V Lowe Collection)*

against enemy aircraft at the airfields they strafed. Indeed, the leading air ace of the French campaign, Hauptmann Wilhelm Balthasar, claimed no fewer than 13 strafing victories in addition to his 23 aerial successes. Again, this was a portent of what was to come.

Impromptu strafing of ground targets by Bf 109 pilots took many forms during the Battle of France, and culminated in attacks of this type during the Dunkirk evacuation in late May and early June 1940. But none of this involved deliberately organised sorties by dedicated units specifically tasked with this type of mission. Rather, it involved 'normal' fighter units taking on ground targets when their usual aerial opponents were absent or held at bay. It was more a case of hitting targets of opportunity when they were available.

The Luftwaffe's dedicated attack assets operated during the *Blitzkrieg* period with mixed success. The Hs 123 proved highly effective where aerial opposition was absent, but was clearly outclassed by modern fighter opposition. The famed and feared Ju 87 proved to be a significant and often decisive weapon in the *Blitzkrieg* doctrines with its precision dive-bombing, but again this was most readily achieved when Allied fighters were not present. But far more worrying for the Luftwaffe, events during the Battle of France proved that the Bf 110 long-range fighter 'destroyer' was only marginally less vulnerable than the Hs 123. The much-vaunted twin-engined Messerschmitt, which was a favourite of the Luftwaffe's commander-in-chief,

Reichsmarschall Hermann Göring, had commenced its operational career in World War 2 with considerable success over Poland. However, when the aircraft came up against French and Royal Air Force (RAF) single-seat fighters during the Battle of France, the Bf 110 had proven significantly vulnerable.

One of the lessons that was learned from experience during the Battle of France was that a viable attack aircraft needed to be fast, well-armed and able to look after itself when faced by good quality aerial opposition. The Luftwaffe operations over France were the first time that German aircraft had faced modern fighters in significant numbers, which was a considerable wake-up call for aircrew and leaders alike. This point was to be further reinforced for the Luftwaffe during the initial phase of the Battle of Britain which commenced in July 1940. The Ju 87 quickly proved to be highly vulnerable to RAF fighters, with significant losses being suffered during several operations. These culminated in two costly days – 16 and 18 August – resulting in the type being removed from frontline operations in the West (although Ju 87s later served with renewed success in the very different operational environments of the Eastern Front and the Mediterranean).

During the spring of 1940 it was becoming obvious to the Luftwaffe's planners that no matter how successful the campaign in France turned out to be, an air war against Britain was highly likely. This obviously created a completely new set of problems.

Up to the time of the defeat of France, support missions in aid of ground forces had been flown over comparatively short distances, directly to assist the infantry and mechanised forces. But it was becoming clear to the Luftwaffe's planners that any war against Britain would of necessity mean an over-water flight across the English Channel, there and back. The distances involved were also greater than anything that had been needed beforehand, even over land. The fighter missions that had been flown thus far during the *Blitzkrieg* era by the Luftwaffe's Bf 109s had been comparatively short-range. The limited amount of air-to-ground work performed by Bf 109 pilots had been largely ad hoc and impromptu when suitable targets had been found.

The Bf 109 was designed as a fighter and was not intended to be a dedicated fighter-bomber. Indeed, at the time of its birth, the concept of fighter-bombers had not even evolved. Therefore, some thought had to go into what would work with its compact airframe in order to develop it into an effective air-to-ground aircraft. One of the possibilities that the Messerschmitt designers examined was the option of mounting a bomb rack beneath the fuselage to carry either a single 250-kg bomb or four 50-kg weapons. In the event, the Bf 109 turned out to be far more versatile than its designers could have thought when it was first conceived.

Manhandling a 250-kg bomb beneath the fuselage of a Bf 109E required the weapon to be brought in from the front on a standard wheeled carrying cradle, two groundcrew being underneath the aircraft ready to locate and fit the ordnance in place (*Malcolm V Lowe Collection*)

RIGHT
The Bf 109E's comparatively short range and endurance was addressed, at least in part, by the development of the means to carry a 300-litre drop tank beneath the fuselage. The first mark to be plumbed from the start of its production to carry this external fuel tank on a specially adapted pylon was the Bf 109E-7, increasing the type's range from some 410 miles (depending on mission profile and climatic conditions) to a much more useful 820 miles. Production of the Bf 109E-7 (all variants) is believed to have numbered 438 examples (*Malcolm V Lowe Collection*)

Development work to turn the Bf 109E fighter into a *Jabo* was accomplished relatively quickly, the tasking being shared between Messerschmitt, technical officers in the RLM and weapons specialists at the Tarnewitz test centre (*EN Archive*)

To begin with, existing examples of the E-series were converted into attack configuration with the installation of an under-fuselage weapons pylon, which could be aimed using the type's existing Revi gunsight. Initial conversions were made to E-1 and E-3 airframes. These obviously differed in wing armament, but this was not considered to be a problem. The first conversions were made in the spring of 1940. Thus modified, the designations Bf 109E-1/B and Bf 109E-3/B were utilised.

An ETC 500 weapons rack for a 250-kg bomb or alternatively an ETC 50 pylon for four 50-kg bombs (the latter holding the bombs in two pairs in tandem) were adapted for fitment beneath the fuselage. For installation in that position on the Bf 109, both racks were effectively new designs, and they were rushed into production as soon as possible. However, these additional 'bumps' reduced the Messerschmitt's top speed by some 7 km/h, and with a bomb carried this could be more than 20 km/h. Such a speed penalty was obviously a great concern to the pilots who would take these aircraft into combat.

Veteran fighter pilot Theodor Osterkamp, one of the Luftwaffe's 'Alter Hasen' (old hares) who had flown in World War 1 and was *Geschwaderkommodore* of JG 51 during 1940, later wrote;

'The Me 109 was not made or at first intended for dropping bombs. Operational needs made it into a fighter that was also a bomber, but it was not an ideal change.'

In what way the bomb or bombs could be most effectively dropped for maximum accuracy using the Bf 109E was a new problem. The type had not been employed in this way before, and indeed – as Osterkamp correctly pointed out – it had not been designed for the fighter-bomber mission. The fact that it could be adapted quite easily for this brand new operational capability was a testament to the type's design and the talented engineers who had created it. However, just how effective the Bf 109E would be as a fast fighter-bomber needed to be tried out, and a number of development airframes were delegated by Messerschmitt for this purpose. One of the aircraft involved was Erla-built Bf 109E-3 Wk-Nr 1361.

For practical purposes, the methods by which the new bomb-carrying Messerschmitt could be best employed in combat would only be solved by an operational deployment of the new fighter-bombers.

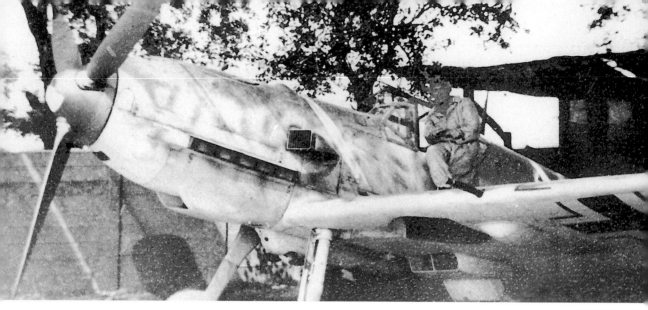

CHAPTER TWO

DEADLY COMBAT

ormed on 1 July 1940 at Köln-Ostheim, *Erprobungsgruppe* (ErprGr) 210 was to become the pioneer of Bf 109 *Jabo* operations. This unit's title was derived from the Messerschmitt Me 210, which was under development as a heavy fighter and fast-attack aircraft as a possible replacement for the Bf 110. It was intended that ErprGr 210 would make the operational evaluation of the type. However, continuing problems with the Me 210, which originally flew in September 1939, resulted in the unit going to war equipped primarily with the Bf 110, its role being adapted to the development of *Jabo* attack and close-support tactics. However, it was ErprGr 210's activities with *Jabo*-configured Bf 109Es rather than the unit's Bf 110C/Ds that were of greatest long-term importance to the Luftwaffe's developing air-to-ground capabilities and strategies.

The *Stab* (headquarters unit) of ErprGr 210 was created from new – 1./ErprGr 210 was re-designated from *Zerstörergeschwader* (ZG) 1's 1. *Staffel*, equipped with Bf 110s; 2./ErprGr 210 derived from *Sturzkampfgeschwader* (StG) 77's 3. *Staffel*, also with Bf 110s; and, significantly for the Bf 109, 3./ErprGr 210 came into being from *Trägergruppe* 186's 4. *Staffel*, and was intended to be equipped with *Jabo* 'Emils'. The *Gruppenkommandeur* of this new specialist organisation was Hauptmann Walter Rubensdörffer.

The Bf 109Es that 3./ErprGr 210 received during July 1940 for its new assignment were primarily Bf 109E-4/B *Jabos* that were under manufacture at that time. In total, 226 E-4s were completed as Bf 109E-4/B *Jabos* (some

The pioneer Bf 109 *Jabo Staffel* was 3./ErprGr 210, headquartered at Denain-Prouvy but forward-based at Calais-Marck for operations over southeast England. Amongst its early aircraft was this ETC rack-equipped Bf 109E-4/B 'Yellow 3', assigned to Unteroffizier August Wiing (seen here sat on the cockpit sill). One of the *Staffel*'s original specialist *Jabo* pilots, Wiing was an experienced aviator who had logged many hours in gliders prior to World War 2. He later served with the experimental test and evaluation unit *Erprobungskommando* 262 during the development of the Me 262 (*EN Archive*)

3./ErprGr 210's Bf 109E fighter-bombers wore a unique style of camouflage that included vertical and diagonal streaks on their otherwise very visible light blue fuselage sides. Many 'Emil' units adopted their own 'in the field' paintwork over the standard factory finishes during the summer of 1940 to make their aircraft less visible to RAF fighters (*Malcolm V Lowe Collection*)

post-war sources claim that the total was 211). Up to 110 Bf 109E-1/Bs were also completed in that way on the production line, there being some over-lapping of manufacturing periods for the different marks of 'Emil' in the factories. Ultimately there were also conversions 'in the field' from standard E-1 and E-3 fighter examples to *Jabo* configuration as well, using kits of parts including the ETC 500 stores carrier. The exact number converted in this way from standard fighter 'Emils' is not known.

The basic Bf 109E-4 fighter started to arrive in numbers for *Jagdwaffe* units during the late spring and early summer of 1940. Some examples were therefore able to take part in the Battle of France, and this version was of great importance during the Battle of Britain, which, according to the RAF, officially commenced on 10 July 1940.

For 3./ErprGr 210, the Bf 109E-4/B was a potentially powerful weapon. Its obvious Achilles' Heel, however, was the Bf 109's acknowledged limited range and endurance. Although Messerschmitt's designers had already been working on the provision for the carriage under the fuselage of a 300-litre drop tank for the 'Emil', this would not appear on the production line until the next major series version – the Bf 109E-7. Armed with the same weapons as the E-4, the E-7 was plumbed for a 300-litre drop tank below the fuselage, or could be fitted with the ETC 500 or ETC 50 bomb rack in the same position – but the fuel tank and bombs could not be carried simultaneously. The designation Bf 109E-7/B is often used for the *Jabo* version, the E-7 being the first to be built from the start of production as a fighter-bomber and to have provision for the 300-litre drop tank.

The working-up by 3./ErprGr 210 on the potent new *Jabo* was intense but effective. Led by Oberleutnant Otto Hintze, the *Staffel* moved to the French airfield of Denain-Prouvy near Valenciennes on 10 July, and immediately put into place training with the new fighter-bombers. This included the development of tactics. It was found for low- to medium-level operations that a dive of roughly 45 degrees at 600 km/h, followed by a slight pull-up to attain level flight during which the bomb was released and lobbed towards its target, was an effective way of delivering the SC 250 250-kg bombs that the unit would be using in combat. For attacks from higher altitudes, a speed of 650 km/h was preferable during the dive.

Believed to have been taken at Denain-Prouvy, this photograph shows a Bf 109E-4/B *Jabo* (or possibly an E-3 conversion) from 3./ErprGr 210 awaiting its next sortie. The ETC 500 rack beneath the fuselage featured four protrusions which could be adjusted to ensure that the 250-kg SC 250 bomb (an example of which is seen here) was carried securely and did not sway when the Messerschmitt made its take-off run or was in flight en route to the target (*Malcolm V Lowe Collection*)

Employing the Messerschmitt's Revi gunsight as a makeshift bombsight was tried out. To give the pilots an indication that they were diving at the correct angle, some aircraft at least (although apparently not all) had a thin red line painted onto the forward transparent panel of their cockpit canopies as a rough visual aid – this was aligned so that it would appear level with the horizon when the correct angle had been attained. This was clearly a much shallower angle than that employed by Ju 87s, but it was sufficient for the mission profile that the Bf 109s were intended to perform.

One of the experienced pilots working on these early tactics was Hauptmann Karl Valesi, who was killed in a training accident following the move to Denain. Practice with concrete bombs proved the potential effectiveness of the new tactics, and within a few days the unit put its ideas to the test.

ANTI-SHIPPING ATTACKS

A number of *Jabo* attacks against shipping targets in the English Channel were commenced, which initially proved the concept. At that time the British were using small convoys consisting of merchantmen and coasters, escorted by small warships, to move goods and equipment. These amounted to superlative targets for the new *Jabos* to prove their worth. The *Staffel* began by flying armed reconnaissance missions over the Channel, usually in *Schwarm* (four-aircraft) formations, escorted by fighter Bf 109Es. Targets of opportunity were attacked, including miscellaneous shipping that the *Jabos* came across. Less heavily defended than shore-based targets, and easier to pick out against the watery background, small ships were the ideal way to begin easing the *Jabo* Messerschmitts into the frontline. During the third week of July, just after the official start of the Battle of Britain, the unit began taking a toll of the maritime targets.

A distinctively camouflaged Bf 109E-3/B *Jabo* probably from 3./ErprGr 210 has its engine run up prior to taxiing out from its well hidden revetment in northern France at the start of another mission. Both the Bf 109E-1/B and E-4B were manufactured on the production line as *Jabos*, whilst a number of standard E-1, E-3 and E-4 fighters were converted into *Jabo*-configuration 'in the field' with the fitment of the ETC 500 bomb carrier beneath the fuselage and the required wiring and control panel in the cockpit (*EN Archive*)

The first big day for 3./ErprGr 210 was 19 July, when the squadron attacked shipping in the Port of Dover alongside the Bf 110s of 1. and 2. *Staffel* of ErprGr 210, escorted by Bf 109Es of III./JG 51. A second attack later that day resulted in the sinking of a small oiler and damage to the G-class destroyer HMS *Griffin* (H31). This success was followed by further anti-shipping missions, with various vessels being attacked.

By the end of the month, the *Gruppe* as a whole had claimed the destruction of some 89,000 tons of shipping. Although this was almost certainly an over-estimate, there was no doubt that these *Jabo* attacks were proving a problem for the British defences, which were having trouble countering the fast-moving, precision strikes. Indeed, with the Luftwaffe's much-vaunted Ju 87 dive-bombers already struggling against defending RAF fighters, ErprGr 210 was proving to be a welcome success in providing a precision strike capability, together with the low-level specialists of 9./KG 76 in their Dornier Do 17Z twin-engined bombers. Indeed, on 30 July, Denain was visited by Generalfeldmarschall Albert Kesselring, the head of *Luftflotte* 2 to which ErprGr 210 was subordinate. He was full of praise for the unit's activities, which were a part of the overall *Kanalkampf* (English Channel Battle) which the Germans were successfully conducting at that time.

Operations were carried out as far as locations such as Harwich, on the Essex coast, where the trawler *Cape Finisterre* was sunk (according to Admiralty records) on 2 August. The Bf 109E *Jabos* were clearly proving their worth, although at that time they were still very small in number.

Targets that were of great importance to the Germans included British radar installations, and these were subjected to a variety of raids, including some attacks that proved costly for the Ju 87 dive-bombers taking part. Emboldened by the continuing anti-shipping successes of the *Kanalkampf*, ErprGr 210's Messerschmitts began striking at land targets, which included these vital radar sites. On 12 August a major raid was mounted, with ErprGr 210's entire operational assets attacking radar sites at Dunkirk (situated on the old Roman Road of Watling Street in Kent) and on the Kentish coast at Pevensey, Rye and Dover. The latter was raided by the *Jabo* Bf 109Es of 3./ErprGr 210, and four sites all suffered some damage, with only Dunkirk managing to stay 'on the air' without interruption.

Later the same day, the Messerschmitts returned, this time in company with the Do 17Z bombers of I./KG 2 from Cambrai-Épinoy. The Dorniers had some difficulty in keeping up with the fast Messerschmitts, whose pilots had to throttle back. Together, they raided Manston airfield in Kent, causing much damage. It was the start of a potentially deadly campaign

against airfields, particularly those of RAF Fighter Command. These were vital to Britain's defence, and they therefore came to be amongst the most important targets for the new Bf 109 *Jabos*. During the following months, RAF airfields often featured amongst the locations attacked by the fighter-bombers.

The successful raid against Manston was followed by a similarly destructive foray against RAF Martlesham Heath airfield in Suffolk on 15 August. Considerable damage was caused during the surprise, low-level attack, but this was stretching the range of the Bf 109s, which in theory was some 410 miles so long as no aerial combat was involved. To alleviate this problem, 3./ErprGr 210 had started to use the forward airfield of Calais-Marck as its operational location. This was nearer to England than Denain, and so gave a little more range and endurance, although the *Jabos* still preferred to avoid any type of aerial combat that would burn fuel and, in any case, could be deadly.

Indeed, that day, 3./ErprGr 210 suffered its first combat loss. Following on from the Martlesham Heath attack, ErprGr 210 intended to raid RAF Kenley, in Surrey, with both Bf 110s and Bf 109Es. However, the *Jabos* missed their target and attacked nearby Croydon airfield instead. This resulted in considerable damage and many civilian casualties in the surrounding areas. Having failed to spot their intended target, the raiders were successfully intercepted by pilots from Nos 32 and 111 Sqns, both units flying Hurricanes.

The vulnerable Bf 110s reacted in the way that they had been taught to and formed defensive circles, which is just what the RAF pilots needed them to do. The Bf 109Es of 3./ErprGr 210 attempted to provide protection, but could not prevent six of the lumbering Bf 110s from being shot down. Included amongst these losses was the aircraft flown by the *Gruppenkommandeur*, Hauptmann Walter Rubensdörffer. The Bf 109E *Jabo* of Leutnant Horst Marx was also shot down by a No 32 Sqn Hurricane. Marx bailed out and survived, his Messerschmitt being destroyed in the

Proving that Bf 109E fighter-bombers carried the comparatively rare ETC 50 bomb rack for four 50-kg bombs beneath the fuselage, and that aircraft of I.(J)/LG 2 did indeed perform *Jabo* sorties in addition to their normal fighter role, this Bf 109E-4B bears the rear fuselage top hat insignia of 2.(J)/LG 2. The four SC 50 bombs featured whistles on their fins to enhance their noise while falling. The 'Emil' was almost certainly photographed at Marquise in October 1940 (*Tony Holmes Collection*) subsequent crash. He was very careful during his subsequent interrogation to avoid giving away the true identity of his aircraft, although it was the first Bf 109E fighter-bomber to fall over England.

Marx had been downed by future ace Plt Off John Layton Flinders. Known to his comrades as 'Polly' Flinders after the 19th century nursery rhyme character, he described the combat as follows;

'An Me 109 came towards me from the starboard side. I throttled back completely and he passed in front of me and into my sights. I fired for about two seconds and a stream of white smoke came from his engine. The aircraft dived towards the ground. A minute later I saw a parachute open at about 6000 ft south of Sevenoaks.'

Overall, the small *Staffel*-strength 3./ErprGr 210 with its fighter-bomber 'Emils' was clearly more successful at *Jabo* operations than the other two Bf 110-equipped *Staffeln* of ErprGr 210, and an expansion in the Bf 109 fighter-bomber force seemed a logical next step. Therefore, although ErprGr 210 was the pioneer in Bf 109 *Jabo* operations over England, it was not to be the only unit to perform this new and specialised mission prior to the conclusion of the Battle of Britain. The eventual partner of ErprGr 210 for Bf 109 *Jabo* raids against English targets was *Lehrgeschwader* (LG) 2. In Luftwaffe parlance the *Lehrgeschwader* has an ambiguous meaning that is sometimes taken to mean an operational training or demonstration unit. However, the two principal *Lehrgeschwader* that existed during the war, LGs 1 and 2, both took on fully operational frontline roles and saw a considerable amount of combat.

LG 2 comprised two very different *Gruppen*, although both flew the Bf 109E. One was a fighter component, the other was a genuine *Jabo* unit. The fighter element was I.(*Jagd*)/LG 2, which had come into being in 1 November 1938 at Garz, in northern Germany, formed from the former *Lehrgeschwader Greifswald* which was the first of the Luftwaffe's LG units. Led by Major Hanns Trübenbach, it was initially equipped with Jumo-engined Bf 109Ds. However, I.(J)/LG 2 became one of the first units to receive Bf 109Es when these started to enter Luftwaffe service in early 1939. During the campaign against Poland in September 1939, it was one of the units that assisted in the operational development of the type. Indeed, the *Gruppe*'s three *Staffeln*, 1., 2. and 3./LG 2, were conventional fighter units.

On the other hand, II.(*Schlacht*)/LG 2 was the attack component of LG 2, and it was destined to play a key role in the use of the *Jabo* Bf 109E during 1940. The *Gruppe* was originally formed on 1 November 1938 at Tutow, in northern Germany. The unit grew out of *Schlachtfliegergruppe* 10, its first commanding officer being Major Georg Spielvogel. II.(S)/LG 2's three component *Staffeln* were 4., 5. and 6./LG 2, which were equipped with the Hs 123. Operating this rugged biplane, II.(S)/LG 2 went to war in September 1939, and used the type throughout the *Blitzkrieg* era of 1939–40. The three *Staffeln* employed their Hs 123s in close-support ground attack operations, as befitted their *Schlacht* (literally 'Battle', but better translated as 'Attack') title.

In principle, the task of the *Lehrgeschwader*'s *Schlacht Gruppe* was the tactical support of ground forces, in addition to its original purpose of the operational development of air-to-ground attack tactics of suitable aircraft and their employment in a combat environment. In other words, the unit's aircraft were intended for comparatively short-range sorties near to the frontlines, and they were not required to fly long distances to strike at strategic targets far distant from any fighting. In that sense, the Hs 123 was the perfect choice, even though it was a slow and potentially highly vulnerable biplane. But as fighter opposition in the early days of World War 2 was not substantial or particularly well coordinated, II.(S)/LG 2 had operated the type with considerable, if largely unheralded, success. This type of close support was an integral part of the *Blitzkrieg* performed in the first nine months or so of World War 2.

The next phase of the war – the onslaught against Britain – was a totally different scenario. The English Channel changed everything. Over-flying water, much longer distances to reach the enemy and the need to strike at 'hard' targets such as industrial complexes rather than ground troops completely transformed the tactical situation that the Luftwaffe now faced. The three *Schlacht Staffeln* of LG 2 now had to be transformed into a different fighting force altogether.

To that end, when the Battle of France concluded on 25 June 1940, II.(S)/LG 2 was withdrawn from its operational base at Cambrai-Épinoy. The unit moved during the latter part of June to Braunschweig-Waggum in Germany for rest and re-equipping with the 'Emil'. During July 1940 the *Gruppe* began receiving the Bf 109E-4/B, which was then in production, although earlier E-models that had been converted to *Jabo* standard were also becoming available. The intention was that it would fly Bf 109E *Jabos* in combat. This would be achieved along the lines of the successful use of the Hs 123 by the unit, but it would also involve integrating them into service and working with the standard Bf 109E fighters of I.(J)/LG 2 to devise tactics that would work best in the expected taxing operational environment of flying against the RAF over distant southern England. In other words, II.(S)/LG 2 would now transition from the *Schlacht* ground-attack to the *Jabo* fighter-bomber mission.

LG 2 also included within its ranks a *Schlacht Ergänzungsstaffel* (training squadron) designated *Erg.Staffel* (*Schlacht*)/LG 2 for the operational indoctrination of pilots newly posted into the *Gruppe*.

As already related, the combat debut of the Bf 109E *Jabos* was achieved by 3./ErprGr 210, although this unit's relatively rapid introduction of the fighter-bomber Messerschmitts into frontline operations was partly caused by the unexpected delays with the service debut of the twin-engined Me 210 which the unit was supposed to be evaluating. However, the arrival of II.(S)/LG 2 with its new Bf 109E-4/Bs on the Channel Front added considerably to the *Jabo* force. Indeed, it was to be this *Gruppe* that became the most high-profile *Jabo* unit during the Battle of Britain.

After a brief stay at Stuttgart-Böblingen for further training, the *Gruppe* moved to Calais-Marck, which was to be its home until the spring of

Hauptmann (later Major) Otto Weiss was the *Gruppenkommandeur* of II.(S)/LG 2 during 1939–40. He had taken over command of the *Gruppe* in late 1939, and duly led it through the *Blitzkrieg* and Battle of Britain. Under his leadership, II.(S)/LG 2 successfully transitioned onto the Bf 109E *Jabo* from its former mount, the Hs 123. Highly decorated, Weiss led the *Gruppe* on the Eastern Front until it became the core of SG 1 in mid-January 1942 – he then became *Geschwaderkommodore* of the newly formed unit. Relieved by Oberstleutnant Hubertus Hitschhold in June 1942, Weiss survived the war (*Malcolm V Lowe Collection*)

Starboard fuselage details of Bf 109E-4/B 'Yellow C' flown by Feldwebel Werner Gottschalk. Assigned to 6.(S)/LG 2, Gottschalk was an early casualty of the *Geschwader*'s operations over England, being forced to land at Hawkinge airfield on 6 September 1940 due to fuel loss after his fighter-bomber was damaged by anti-aircraft fire when he strayed too close to the naval dockyard at Chatham (*Malcolm V Lowe Collection*)

1941. By then, II.(S)/LG 2 was commanded by Hauptmann Otto Weiss. Its big day was 2 September 1940. Now declared fully operational within *Luftflotte* 2, the *Gruppe* undertook its first sorties during a day of raids by the Luftwaffe against various targets in Kent and the Thames Estuary. Alerted, the British defences successfully drove off these attacks, with LG 2's fighters and *Jabos* suffering no casualties.

With II.(S)/LG 2 thus committed, a growing number of missions were subsequently flown as the scope and scale of Bf 109E *Jabo* operations was increased. However, it was not long before the British had the chance to examine one of LG 2's *Jabos*. A 6 September mission resulted in the loss of Feldwebel Werner Gottschalk of 6./LG 2 and his Bf 109E-4/B 'Yellow C'. Flying as escort to other *Jabos* of II./LG 2, Gottschalk came under fire from ground defences around the heavily defended Chatham naval dockyard and landed at Hawkinge airfield, on the Kent coast, much to the surprise of the local anti-aircraft gunners. With Gottschalk's fighter-bomber being practically intact, the aircraft proved to be of great interest to the British as it was the first complete Bf 109E *Jabo* to be captured.

A second II./LG 2 fighter-bomber was lost that day. Also hit by ground fire in the vicinity of Chatham, Leutnant Herbert Dültgen bailed out of his stricken *Jabo*, which crashed into the sea near The Nore sandbank in the Thames Estuary.

British defences were not the only hazard facing the *Jabo* pilots. The *Jagdflieger* (pilots of the Luftwaffe's fighter arm) flying Bf 109Es over England were already keenly aware that dogfighting with RAF fighters if intercepted used up a lot of precious fuel. The conversion of Bf 109Es into *Jabos* put more pressure on this fine balance – the extra weight and drag exerted by carrying an SC 250 bomb to a target increased fuel consumption on the outward journey even without the possibility of meeting enemy fighters in the air. To that end, the *Jabos* were highly reluctant to engage in aerial combat with RAF fighters, even though on paper they were more than capable of looking after themselves once they had delivered their ordnance. Very often, *Jabo* raids had fighter escort, although the exact format of the *Jabo* missions was an evolving strategy. Sometimes, the *Jabos* had no escort, whilst at other times the escort from standard fighter units could be very thorough.

The potential 'fix' to the Bf 109E's perennial range/endurance problems for operations against southern England was the Bf 109E-7, which was plumbed from the start to be able to carry a 300-litre drop tank beneath the fuselage. The first E-7s reached fighter units on the Channel Front during August 1940.

Joining II.(S)/LG 2 at Calais-Marck were the Bf 109E fighters of I.(J)/LG 2. This *Gruppe* was led at that time by Oberleutnant Herbert Ihlefeld, and numbered amongst its ranks in addition to E-4s some of the new E-7 fighters that could also be used as fighter-bombers, in addition to being equipped to carry the 300-litre underfuselage drop tank. Often, I.(J)/LG 2 escorted the dedicated *Jabos* of II.(S)/LG 2, although sometimes the pilots of I.(J)/LG 2 performed *Jabo* sorties themselves, and vice versa. Included amongst the pilots of I.(J)/LG 2 was future high-scoring ace Fähnrich Hans-Joachim Marseille, who was assigned during August 1940. He later flew Bf 109s in action over North Africa with JG 27, gaining the nickname the 'Star of Africa' before his death in September 1942.

On 31 August, the first of the new Bf 109E-7 fighters to be shot down over southern England was lost in aerial combat. Flown by Oberleutnant Hasso von Perthes of 3(J)./LG 2, E-7 Wk-Nr 5600 was on a bomber escort mission when it was attacked by Plt Off Mirosław Ferić of No 303 Sqn, based at Northolt in west London. He died from his injuries on 14 September. This was the first day that the Polish-manned fighter unit with its Hurricanes was officially operational. The Poles claimed four Bf 109Es of LG 2 shot down on the 31st.

MAJOR TRANSFORMATION

It was on 2 September that the now infamous announcements were made by Reichsmarschall Hermann Göring regarding the need for each *Jagdgeschwader* to convert three of its *Staffeln* into dedicated *Jabo* units. When this suggested major alteration to the pursuit of the air war reached the frontline units, there was a very mixed reaction.

It was clear that the small number of *Jabos* thus far committed by ErprGr 210 and the newly arrived II.(S)/LG 2 were enjoying some

On public display in Preston, Lancashire, Bf 109E-4/B Wk-Nr 3726 'Yellow M' of 6.(S)/LG 2 appears to have attracted only minimal attention. The aircraft's engine and both fuel tanks had been hit by fire from a Spitfire that attacked out of the sun on 5 October 1940. When the DB 601 failed shortly thereafter, Battle of France veteran Feldwebel Erhardt Pankratz force-landed at Peasmarsh. He was immediately taken prisoner (*Andy Saunders Collection*)

This 'bombed up' Bf 109E-4/B *Jabo* of II.(S)/LG 2 features 4. *Staffel*'s 'Mickey Mouse' insignia on its engine cowling. 4./LG 2 was one of the three *Staffeln* within II. *Gruppe* that flew the Bf 109E *Jabo* in combat during the Battle of Britain and its immediate aftermath (*EN Archive*)

success. However, in the coming weeks, Göring became increasingly impatient with his fighter units of the hitherto successful *Jagdwaffe*. The expected defeat of the RAF had not taken place, and the standard fighters were too embroiled in providing escort for the Luftwaffe's twin-engined bombers prior to and during that period for there to be much time or enthusiasm for converting up to a third of the already hard-pressed single-engined fighter force into fighter-bombers.

However, there was also some good sense behind the Reichsmarschall's decision-making. Clearly, the *Jabos* of 3./ErprGr 210 had achieved some remarkable results thus far, even bearing in mind their very limited numbers. It therefore seemed logical for an enlarging of fighter-bomber activities and the conversion of more units onto the type. But in making this decision, Göring had not borne in mind the fact that 3./ErprGr 210's *Jabo* pilots were experienced in fighter-bomber practices and tactics, hence their successes relative to the small number of aircraft that were actually being committed to combat. And, crucially, he missed the point that these airmen were dedicated to their particular trade.

Forcing standard fighter units to convert a third of their strength into *Jabo* squadrons without the necessary training for their pilots was a bad move. It was very unpopular amongst many airmen who found themselves being switched from their accepted job of aerial combat against RAF fighters to the completely new role of *Jabo* bomber pilot. Many seasoned *Jagdflieger*, experienced in air-to-air combat, were thoroughly unimpressed at the idea of having to become *Kampfflieger* virtually overnight.

Some of those in higher authority were similarly unhappy. The veteran fighter pilot Generalmajor Theo Osterkamp, who had led the Bf 109E-equipped JG 51 during the *Blitzkrieg* period and into the early stages of the Battle of Britain, had been moved from his role as *Geschwaderkommodore* to become the *Jagdfliegerführer* (commander) of the fighter units in *Luftflotte* 2 (*Jafü 2*) during the latter part of the Battle. He was unenthusiastic about the decision to make fighter pilots deliver bombs;

'The order for each *Geschwader* to form its own *Jabo Staffeln* came from the highest level. We were left to sort it out ourselves. There was great concern amongst many of us that this was going to be difficult to achieve, and it would distract from our main purpose.'

He was also apprehensive about the morale of his pilots;

'I could already see that some of my fighter leaders, and their over-worked airmen, were unhappy with these changes.'

In the event, each *Jagdgeschwader* nominated a *Staffel* within their constituent three *Gruppen* to comply with the new requirement. Amongst the *Geschwader* that duly reconfigured constituent *Staffeln* to *Jabo* squadrons were the following – JG 3 (2., 5. and 7. *Staffeln*); JG 26

(3., 4. and 9. *Staffeln*); JG 27
(6. and 7. *Staffeln*); JG 51 (2., 5.
and 9. *Staffeln*); JG 53 (3., 4. and
8. *Staffeln)*; JG 54 (6., 8. and 9.
Staffeln); and JG 77 (1. *Staffel*). The
latter, 1./JG 77, was re-designated
10./JG 51 during November 1940.
Not every *Geschwader* found three
suitable *Staffeln*, JG 27, for example,
eventually only reconfiguring two.

Several of these units were
enthusiastic about becoming *Jabo*
squadrons, some less so. Indeed, it
appears that there was a reluctance
on the part of some *Geschwader*
commanders to follow instructions
and convert three of their cherished fighter *Staffeln* into fighter-bomber
units, especially when they were so badly needed for the aerial fighting role.

The new fighter-bomber units were put into action in a great hurry,
and there was barely time to give some of the pilots adequate bombing
training. Indeed, some *Jagdflieger* only had the chance to drop one or two
practice concrete bombs before releasing their first live ordnance in a raid
over London or on other targets in England.

Within JG 2, 2., 6. and 7. *Staffeln* became *Jabo* units, and their activities
are covered in the following chapter because they were not involved
in the Battle of Britain or its immediate aftermath. Indeed, it was not
until November that pilots of 2./JG 2 were initially posted to Denain to
work with 3./ErprGr 210 and LG 2 to commence their conversion onto
fighter-bombers, only becoming operational several months later.

A further problem with the re-purposing of fighter squadrons to
fighter-bomber units was that these *Jabo* aircraft then needed escorting,
particularly on their way to their targets while bomb-carrying. At that
time the standard *Geschwader* were already expected to escort Luftwaffe
twin-engined bombers that were undertaking the majority of raids
mounted against targets well inland in southern England. The likelihood
that yet more escort duty would fall to the already busy fighter pilots was
not greeted with enthusiasm. The escort flying that was being carried out
for the twin-engined bombers was seriously limiting the Bf 109E's already
restricted range and endurance over the British mainland.

Instead of being able to stay and fight it out with RAF fighters, the
Jagdflieger were often having to turn for home rather than engaging in
combat for any length of time. The arrival of the Bf 109E-7 with its
300-litre drop tank beneath the fuselage certainly helped to alleviate this
situation, but did not completely solve the problem.

The singularly unhappy Adolf Galland described a typical mission
profile for his JG 26 in his autobiography *The First and the Last*;

'The fighter-bomber raids were carried out in the following way –
each wing provided the escort for its own bombers. The altitude for the
approach was about 18,000ft. At the start, we let the fighter-bombers
fly in bomber formation, but it was soon apparent that the enemy

Oberleutnant Walter Rupp, *Staffelkapitän*
of 3./JG 53, force-landed his Bf 109E-4B
on Manston airfield after one of his
radiators was holed by a Spitfire off
Gravesend on 17 October 1940. Rupp was
taken prisoner and his aircraft was
salvaged and put on public display. His
unit was one of the fighter *Staffeln* that
was transformed into a *Jabo* squadron on
the orders of Reichsmarschall Göring,
Rupp being one of a number of ranking
Jabo officers to be lost during the final
phase of the Battle of Britain (*Malcolm V
Lowe Collection*)

Oberstleutnant Adolf Galland, *Geschwaderkommodore* of JG 26 and a veteran of fighter-bomber operations with the He 51 in Spain, was unhappy about the Bf 109E being turned into a *Jabo* halfway through the *Battle of Britain*. He commented post-war, 'The fighter pilots were annoyed at carrying "cargo", and were glad to get rid of the bomb anywhere' (*Tony Holmes Collection*)

fighters could concentrate fully on them. Therefore, we distributed the fighter-bombers in small units throughout the entire formation, and thus brought them in fairly safely over their target area. This type of raid had no more than nuisance value. The passive behaviour toward enemy fighters, the feeling of inferiority when we were attacked because of loss of speed, manoeuvrability and rate of climb, added to the unconvincing effect of single bombs scattered over wide areas, combined to ruin the morale of the German fighter pilot, which was already low because of the type of escorting that had to be done.'

Nevertheless, some units did manage to reinvent themselves successfully as fighter-bomber squadrons, which allowed *Jabo* activities to considerably expand. One of the early converts was 9./JG 54, which had started flying limited *Jabo* sorties before the end of September. This was a welcome fillip to the campaign, which was still relying heavily on 3./ErprGr 210 and II.(S)/LG 2, although the overall picture was to change considerably during October due to a significant expansion in the number of *Jabo* units being declared operational.

With sufficient Bf 109E-1/B and E-4/B bomb-carriers reaching frontline units, enough aircraft were on strength to permit a large-scale *Jabo* campaign to be launched. This was delayed due to bad weather at the start of October, allowing more units to have the time to convert themselves into fighter-bomber outfits. However, training for many of the pilots was rudimentary. By that time, RAF Fighter Command's airmen were aware of the capabilities of the bomb-carrying Messerschmitts, and the fact that they would have to turn for home rapidly once they had dropped their bomb due to the range and endurance issues of their 'Emils'. Adolf Galland was particularly dismayed about the lack of training;

'The fighter-bombers were put into action in a great hurry. There was hardly time to give the pilots bombing training. Most pilots dropped their first live bomb in a raid over London or on other targets in England.'

October 1940 would eventually see the height of Bf 109 *Jabo* activity in the West. With several *Staffeln* across a number of *Geschwader* converted to fighter-bomber units to add to the existing 3./ErprGr 210 and II.(S)/LG 2, larger raids were by then a possibility. For some units, however, the start of fighter-bomber operations showed how dangerous these missions could be. Oberleutnant Walter Fiel, the *Staffelkapitän* of 8.(*Jabo*)/JG 53, was lost together with three other aircraft from that unit during the *Staffel's* baptism of fire in the fighter-bomber role on 2 October. He became a PoW, and was replaced by Hauptmann Ernst-Günther Heinze.

An especially significant loss took place on 7 October when Oberleutnant Victor Mölders, brother of the famous fighter ace and tactician Werner Mölders, was brought down and captured during a *Jabo* raid on London.

The *Staffelkapitän* of 2.(*Jabo*)/JG 51 (another of the *Staffeln* that had recently reconfigured from fighter into the fighter-bomber role), Mölders had dropped his 250-kg bomb and rapidly changed course to return as quickly as possible to France when he and his fellow pilots were intercepted by Hurricanes of Nos 501 and 605 Sqns. A running battle ensued until Mölders force landed his *Jabo* Bf 109E-4/B Wk-Nr 4103 'Black 1' near Winchelsea and Guestling, in East Sussex. Three more Messerschmitts were shot down, including a second 'Emil' from 2.(*Jabo*)/JG 51.

As had been the case on the 7th, London was the principal focus of fighter-bomber attacks during October 1940. The relative lull in *Jabo* activity in September was very rapidly reversed now that more *Jagdgeschwader* had converted dedicated *Staffeln* to this role. However, one of the reasons for London being chosen as the main (but not exclusive) focus of *Jabo* activity was that it was a relatively easy target for the inexperienced fighter-bomber pilots to find. This somewhat nullified the initial purpose of the whole *Jabo* mission, which was to strike with precision at high-value military targets. By that time major fires were almost a daily occurrence in the capital, the attendant smoke allowing visual identification to be made by even the most novice pilots.

In essence, the numbers involved in the October *Jabo* strikes were impressive, including the many sorties that were aimed specifically at London. The first major attack took place on the 12th, with several waves of fighter-bombers confounding the British defences. Some 175 aircraft out of the 217 that were despatched targeted the capital. This was repeated on 15 and 17 October, the *Jabos* again mainly bombing London. Considerable damage was inflicted on the capital, with the British defences split by the various waves of *Jabos* sent at different times during the day, mixed in with the on-going sorties by the twin-engined Luftwaffe bombers. This short-lived but destructive campaign continued on several other days in October, including the 25th, when 237 *Jabo* sorties were recorded. This was completely different to the small-scale attacks by just a few *Jabos* against specific pin-point targets that had taken place earlier in the Battle of Britain.

According to Luftwaffe records, 140 separate attacks were made against London during the month by Bf 109 *Jabos*, including 2633 individual sorties – a staggering amount compared to the small beginnings of the Bf 109 fighter-bomber contingent at the start of the Battle of Britain. The campaign against London during the latter part of October 1940 was truly the peak of the Bf 109's activities as a *Jabo* in the West. Significant raids had been undertaken, with the British defences finding it difficult to counter these large-scale attacks that were flown in conjunction with other twin- and single-engined fighter operations.

But in effect the fighter-bomber campaign against London represented a wasteful use of the *Jabos*. Many more precision attacks in large numbers against genuinely high-value military targets such as airfields and radar sites would have been a far better use of the *Jabos*. Simply pounding London, which was already being attacked by Luftwaffe twin-engined bombers during the day and increasingly at night as the nocturnal *Blitz* increased in intensity, was a far less useful way to employ the comparatively sizeable fighter-bomber force that was eventually created. Precision attacks on airfields and other vital military and infrastructure targets caused considerable damage, but this was not followed up by enough further raids to make a real dent in Britain's defences. If these attacks had been pursued in greater volume, the outcome of the Battle of Britain could have been more in the balance.

DANGEROUS OPERATIONS

Some *Jabo* losses were spectacular, but fatal for their pilots. On 15 October Leutnant Ludwig Lenz of *Stab* I.(J)/LG 2 was engaged in a *Jabo* sortie when his aircraft was hit during a dogfight, the details of which still remain unclear. It was not known if the Messerschmitt was carrying a 250-kg bomb or a fuel-filled drop tank beneath the fuselage. In any case the ordnance exploded, killing the pilot and scattering wreckage over a roughly three-mile area. The cockpit area and wings landed at Spruce Lawns in Elham, near to Folkestone on the Kent coast .

Crash sites such as this were of great interest to the British. Subsequent to an enemy aircraft's coming down either in one piece or scattered over a wide area, the standard procedure was for an RAF Technical Intelligence Officer from the Air Intelligence 1(g) Department to inspect the wreck, and fill in a 'Form C'. On this document would be recorded data regarding the technical details of the aircraft and its equipment, any information that could be found about its crew, and its markings and insignia, including unit badges and specific unit colourings such as spinner colours. Any live weaponry would be removed as soon as possible.

The wreck would be guarded by either British Army or Home Guard personnel, although this often failed to prevent souvenir hunters from removing components. Once inspected, the wreck then needed to be cleared, a task that fell in the south of England from Hampshire eastwards to personnel of the RAF's No 49 Maintenance Unit (MU). This was based

On 15 October Leutnant Ludwig Lenz of *Stab* I.(J)/LG 2 was killed and his aircraft destroyed when its underfuselage ordnance (either a 250-kg bomb or fuel-filled drop tank) exploded after taking a direct hit from ground fire. The blast scattered wreckage over a roughly three-mile area. The cockpit and wings landed at Spruce Lawns, just north of Elham near to Folkestone in Kent. The *Jabo* was marked with a chevron, confirming its allocation to the *Stab*. Although Lenz's aircraft is sometimes described as a Bf 109E-7, its Wk-Nr, 3734, suggests that it was a Messerschmitt Regensburg-built E-4 (*Andy Saunders Collection*)

at RAF Faygate near Horsham, in West Sussex. Originally entitled No 1 Salvage Centre, the unit was located at Faygate from late September 1939. A team from No 49 MU would remove all parts of the crashed aircraft, and during the Battle of Britain the area around the unit's buildings at Faygate became increasingly filled with wrecked Luftwaffe aircraft and components.

Eventually, civilian contractors were enlisted to help with the task of collecting Luftwaffe aircraft from crash sites due to the number of wrecks that needed to be removed. Finally, much of the metalwork accumulated at Faygate was scrapped and melted down. A similar fate did not await intact German aircraft, which would go on display around the country and overseas or, in a small number of cases, were made airworthy again.

II.(S)/LG 2 and 3./ErprGr 210 often operated together, these two specialist units working as a team from 15 October as an impromptu *Gruppe*, with both continuing to be located at Calais-Marck. On 29 October Bf 109E-4/Bs of II.(S)/LG 2 mounted a successful *Jabo* strike against North Weald airfield, in Essex – a key RAF Fighter Command base in No. 11 Group. The raid took place under low cloud cover at approximately 1630 hrs, with II./LG 2 joined by 3./ErprGr 210.

The attack on North Weald showed the professionalism of the *Jabo* pilots from these two units, compared to the relative inexperience (and in some cases lack of enthusiasm) of the airmen in the *Jabo*-reconfigured *Staffeln* of the standard fighter *Geschwader*. The raid was carried out from around 3000 ft by some 20 aircraft, the Messerschmitts diving to approximately 500 ft and lobbing their bombs accurately onto the airfield just as Hurricanes of Nos 249 and 257 Sqns were taking off to intercept the attackers. The incoming *Jabos* had been spotted by radar, but their eventual destination remained unclear until the last moment. The 'Emil' pilots succeeded in destroying one of the hangars on the airfield plus the newly re-built guardroom, and the main runway was also holed. A lot of damage was caused, but the death toll was of greatest concern – some 20 personnel were killed and double that number wounded.

The Messerschmitts departed from the target rapidly, expecting to be picked up by their intended escort of Bf 109Es from III./JG 26. However, before they could be safely shepherded away from danger, No 249 Sqn bore down on the *Jabo* pilots, catching them over the Blackwater Estuary. In the major dogfight that ensued, three of the 'Emils' were shot down.

Sgt George Stroud engaged in a long chase that ended 12 miles over the water when he caught and shot down Oberleutnant Bruno von Schenk,

Bf 109E-4/B 'White N' of Oberfeldwebel Josef Harmeling of 4.(S)/LG 2 was hit more than 70 times by a pursuing Hurricane flown by Pole Sgt Michał Maciejowski of No 249 Sqn as the *Jabo* fled at 3000 ft after its low-level bombing raid against London on 29 October. With both radiators holed and his engine overheating, Harmeling had to force land his *Jabo* at Langenhoe, in Essex. The damaged airframe subsequently toured Britain, being shown to the public for fund-raising and educational purposes in various towns and cities (*Andy Saunders Collection*)

The desolate, flattened remains of Bf 109E-4/B Wk-Nr 5562 'White B' from 4.(S)/LG 2, flown by Unteroffizier Hans-Joachim Rank, near Goldhanger, Essex. The aircraft was shot down at 1645 hrs on 29 October by Flt Lt R A 'Butch' Barton of No 249 Sqn shortly after attacking North Weald airfield. Although Rank succeeded in bailing out, he succumbed to his wounds several hours later (*Andy Saunders Collection*)

the *Staffelkapitän* of 5.(S)/LG 2, who did not survive the encounter. Oberfeldwebel Josef Harmeling of 4.(S)/LG 2 had to force land his *Jabo* at Langenhoe, Essex, brought down by Polish pilot Sgt Michał Maciejowski. Also from 4.(S)/LG 2, Unteroffizier Hans-Joachim Rank was shot down at 1645 hrs by Flt Lt Robert Alexander 'Butch' Barton. Rank bailed out of his damaged aircraft (Bf 109E-4/B Wk-Nr 5562 'White B'), which crashed and was totally destroyed beside the B1062 minor road at Charity Farm near Goldhanger, Essex. The pilot had been badly burned and wounded in the right thigh, and even though he was rushed to hospital in Maldon, he died soon after.

Twelve-year-old Cyril Southgate witnessed Rank's demise, and he later recorded his memories for a local history project in Goldhanger;

'Still clear in my mind is the crash of an ME 109 fighter 100 yards west of Charity Farm cottages, on the Maldon Road just out of the village. The pilot of this particular aircraft parachuted out and landed at Sheepcotes Farm, Little Totham. He was badly burned and died [in hospital] that night. He was initially buried in Maldon cemetery and later re-buried in the German war graves cemetery at Cannock Chase in Staffordshire'.

A replacement for von Schenk as the leader of 5.(S)/LG 2 was rapidly found in Oberleutnant Georg Dörffel.

ErprGr 210 also suffered a major setback on 29 October when the *Staffelkapitän* of 3./ErprGr 210, Oberleutnant Otto Hintze, was shot down on a *Jabo* mission to London and became a POW. It was his 52nd sortie as a fighter-bomber pilot. Hintze was succeeded by Oberleutnant Peter Emmerich.

Not all losses were due to enemy action. On 30 November, Unteroffizier Paul Wacker of 4.(S)/LG 2 was approaching the Dorset coast near Swanage in his Bf 109E-1/B Wk-Nr 6313 'White G'. Applying engine boost, Wacker must have been surprised and more than a little disappointed when the DB 601 completely failed. With no chance to return across the Channel, Wacker skilfully belly landed his stricken Messerschmitt near

the historic ruin of Corfe Castle. The aircraft was subsequently examined, its airframe being largely undamaged. It was even possible to put the *Jabo* back onto its undercarriage.

Shipped to the US, the aircraft made an excellent exhibit during a subsequent tour, where it generated a large amount of public interest. It appears from several Press reports in the US that parts from other crashed Messerschmitts were used to 'make up' the airframe after some components went missing, and the 'Emil' was displayed without a spinner and propeller unit.

Another experienced *Staffelkapitän* who was lost near to the end of *Jabo* operations in the final weeks of 1940 was Oberleutnant Heinrich Vogler of 4.(S)/LG 2. On 5 December he did not return from an anti-shipping *Jabo* mission while attacking Royal Navy minesweepers in the English Channel. His replacement was Oberleutnant Alfred Druschel. This meant that the only commanding officer of a dedicated *Jabo Staffel* of 3./ErprGr 210 and II.(S)/LG 2 to serve continuously during this period was Oberleutnant Werner Dörnbrack of 6.(S)/LG 2.

The final loss of a Bf 109E *Jabo* during 1940 is generally accepted to have been Oberleutnant Viktor Kraft of *Stab* II.(S)/LG 2 on 11 December. Flying Bf 109E-7/B Wk-Nr 5941 'Green D', he was shot down during a two-aeroplane mission to bomb the London docks. Finding unexpectedly good weather on approach to the capital, the two pilots realised that they would be easily sighted and caught by any patrolling fighters. His wingman turned for France, but Kraft unwisely continued.

By that stage in the war, small numbers of incoming intruders were easy to counteract, especially as Kraft and his wingman had approached at approximately 5000 ft, which made them readily detectable by radar. Kraft was intercepted by Spitfires of No 66 Sqn, based at Biggin Hill in

The forlorn-looking wreck of Unteroffizier Paul Wacker's Bf 109E-1/B Wk-Nr 6313 'White G' of 4.(S)/LG 2 following its belly landing near Corfe Castle, Dorset, on 30 November 1940. The aircraft was lost due to engine failure, and not as a result of enemy action. Wacker was captured, while his aircraft eventually became something of a celebrity (*Malcolm V Lowe Collection*)

Unteroffizier Wacker's Bf 109E-1/B was repaired to static display condition and shipped to the US. It is seen here under guard, the aircraft becoming a prize exhibit on a fund-raising and educational tour in several American locations. During this time it 'inherited' parts from other crashed 'Emils', but was never apparently fitted with a propeller unit and spinner (*Malcolm V Lowe Collection*)

A series of propaganda photographs were taken of this Bf 109E-1/B (or possibly a later model with its wing cannon removed), 'Black 2', in early 1941. The *Jabo* was camouflaged with an unusually heavy mottle on its fuselage sides, suggesting that it had been given a full re-paint. It has been claimed that this *Jabo* belonged to the training unit *Ergänzungsgruppe*/JG 51, based at Cazaux (*Malcolm V Lowe Collection*)

Kent. He was shot down by Plt Off Hubert Raymond Allen, Kraft bailing out and the Messerschmitt crashing into the Kent countryside.

Behind the scenes, the arguments concerning the use of *Jabo* Bf 109Es grew more vociferous as the Battle of Britain drew to a close, and the Luftwaffe took stock of the situation. Adolf Galland in *The First and The Last*, echoing the thoughts of a growing number of his fellow fighter leaders, had this to say;

'We had an outspoken antipathy for the order to escort fighter-bombers. The Luftwaffe High Command countered our negative attitude sharply. Göring declared angrily that the fighter arm had failed to give adequate protection to the bomber squadrons, and that they were now opposed to escorting fighter-bombers – a job which had resulted entirely from their own failure. If they were to prove unfit for this task as well, it would be better to disband the fighter arm altogether. That was the limit!

'The fighter pilots who took part in the Battle of Britain were quite justly convinced that they had done their duty during the past weeks of heavy fighting. They had accepted heavy losses in unflagging action combined with outstanding successes, but never once did they question the final aim or how long this murderous battle was going to last. Morale, having already been heavily taxed, and on top of that to be unjustly accused, put military discipline to a stiff test. In young flying officer circles, the leadership was passionately and bitterly criticised. This was the first serious crisis in the relations between the fighter arm and the Luftwaffe High Command.'

By the end of 1940, the scale and importance of Bf 109E *Jabo* raids on the Channel Front had thus diminished to virtually nothing. Following the high-point of October, *Jabo* activity gradually dwindled from the following month onwards. The considerable strategic advantage that had been gained by the pinpoint *Jabo* attacks against high-value military targets during the Battle of Britain period was thus all-but wasted. Continuing changes to the conduct of the air war from the highest level of the Luftwaffe that had eventually put the greatest emphasis on night attacks by twin-engined bombers had made the *Jabos* virtually redundant by the end of 1940. Their penny-packet raids that persisted into December were by then achieving very little. The Germans, in creating the fighter-bomber concept, had not recognised its full capability.

Interestingly, however, the potential role of the fighter-bomber was soon acknowledged by the British and, ultimately, by their American allies. When the RAF commenced its own offensive over the occupied countries of Western Europe from early 1941 onwards, a significant part of the new campaign included fighters undertaking both bomber escort and air-to-ground operations. It was not just simply a case of fitting heavier calibre guns or cannon to existing fighters such as the Spitfire. A whole generation of powerful fighters that were excellent in air-to-ground operations was eventually developed. Aircraft types such as the Hawker Typhoon and Tempest V and the Republic P-47 Thunderbolt were adherents to the combined fighter and fighter-bomber design concept and served the Allies very well later in the war.

In any case, many of the *Jagdgeschwader* that had participated in the Battle of Britain were being withdrawn from the Channel Front in late 1940 and early 1941. One of the operational factors was the onset of bad weather, which severely curtailed the pursuit of meaningful operations. Some of the units that had fought in the Battle of Britain had been in almost continuous action for many months, even before the start of the Battle. They needed a rest, replenishment and re-equipment. One of the main participants in *Jabo* operations, II.(S)/LG 2, although continuing to operate on the Channel Front for the time being, had barely a dozen serviceable Bf 109E fighter-bombers at the start of 1941.

As a backdrop to these unit-level developments, and to put them into context in the 'bigger picture', the strategic thinking behind Germany's pursuit of World War 2 was also undergoing significant changes by late 1940. This was ultimately to result in the further run-down of Luftwaffe units in the West. Failure in the Battle of Britain to conquer, or at least subdue, the RAF had been a significant factor in the decision at the highest level to postpone the planned invasion. Instead, German strategy irrevocably turned towards the east and war against the Soviet Union.

Within the *Jagdgeschwader* which had formed *Jabo Staffeln* following Göring's order to reconfigure fighter squadrons into *Jabo* units, there was a general reversion back to the fighter role of these *Staffeln* when the *Geschwader* returned to Germany.

This Bf 109E-1/B bore the markings style of one of the *Jabo Staffeln* of JG 27, and is believed to have been photographed at Bad Zwischenahn, in Germany, when the *Jagdgeschwader* withdrew from the Channel Front in late 1940. The weapon beneath its fuselage hanging from the ETC 500 bomb rack is an inert practice training round, denoted by the light-coloured paintwork on its nose (*Malcolm V Lowe Collection*)

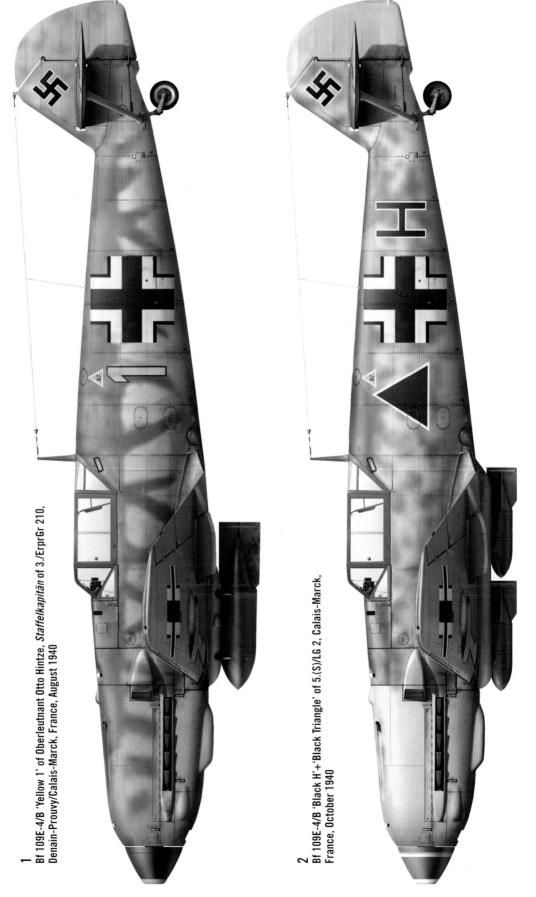

COLOUR PLATES

1
Bf 109E-4/B 'Yellow 1' of Oberleutnant Otto Hintze, *Staffelkapitän* of 3./ErprGr 210, Denain-Prouvy/Calais-Marck, France, August 1940

2
Bf 109E-4/B 'Black H' + 'Black Triangle' of 5.(S)/LG 2, Calais-Marck, France, October 1940

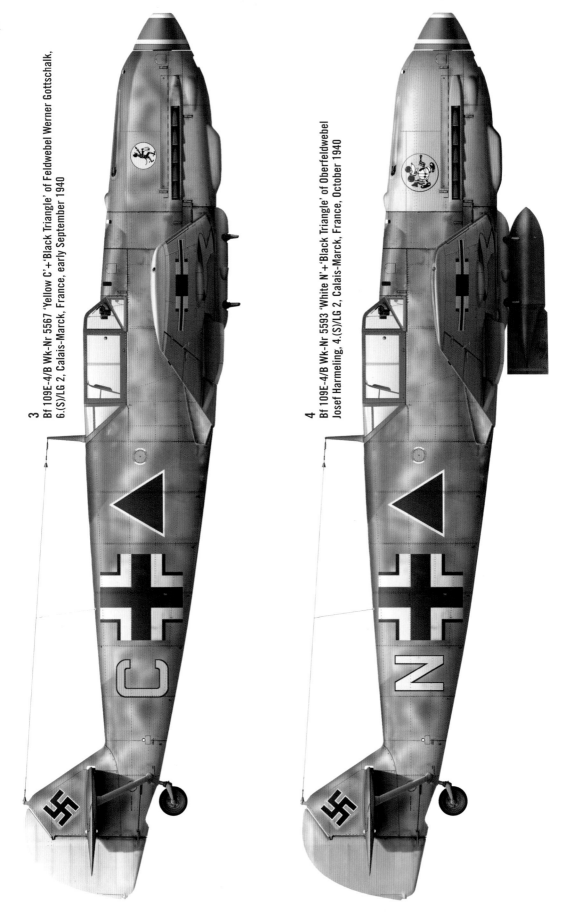

3
Bf 109E-4/B Wk-Nr 5567 'Yellow C' + 'Black Triangle' of Feldwebel Werner Gottschalk,
6.(S)/LG 2, Calais-Marck, France, early September 1940

4
Bf 109E-4/B Wk-Nr 5593 'White N' + 'Black Triangle' of Oberfeldwebel
Josef Harmeling, 4.(S)/LG 2, Calais-Marck, France, October 1940

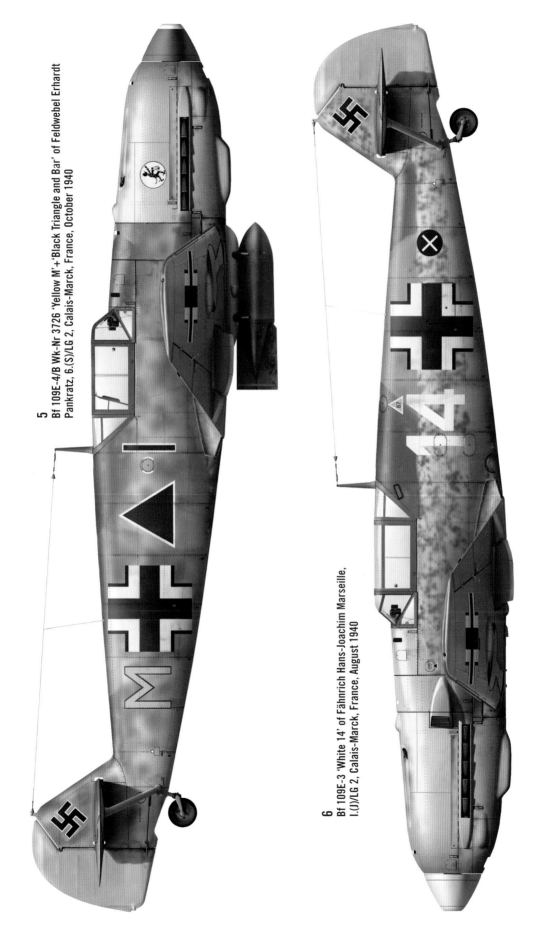

5
Bf 109E-4/B Wk-Nr 3726 'Yellow M' + 'Black Triangle and Bar' of Feldwebel Erhardt Pankratz, 6.(S)/LG 2, Calais-Marck, France, October 1940

6
Bf 109E-3 'White 14' of Fähnrich Hans-Joachim Marseille, I.(J)/LG 2, Calais-Marck, France, August 1940

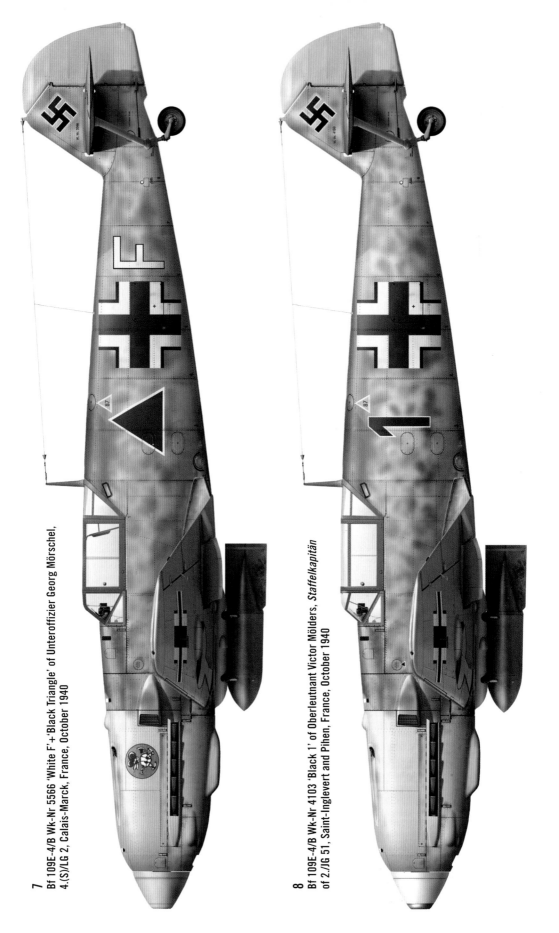

7
Bf 109E-4/B Wk-Nr 5566 'White F' + 'Black Triangle' of Unteroffizier Georg Mörschel, 4.(S)/LG 2, Calais-Marck, France, October 1940

8
Bf 109E-4/B Wk-Nr 4103 'Black 1' of Oberleutnant Victor Mölders, *Staffelkapitän* of 2./JG 51, Saint-Inglevert and Pihen, France, October 1940

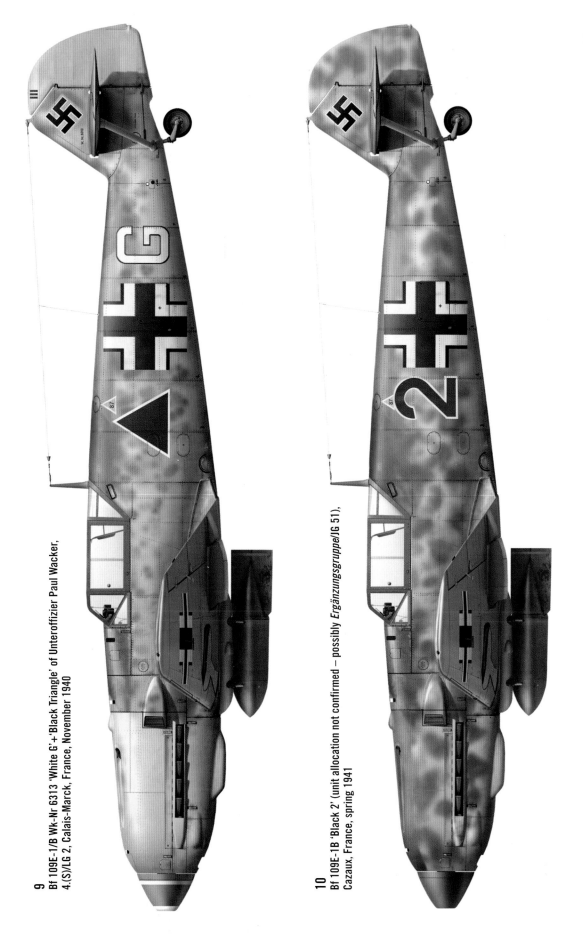

9
Bf 109E-1/B Wk-Nr 6313 'White G' + 'Black Triangle' of Unteroffizier Paul Wacker, 4.(S)/LG 2, Calais-Marck, France, November 1940

10
Bf 109E-1B 'Black 2' (unit allocation not confirmed – possibly *Ergänzungsgruppe*/JG 51), Cazaux, France, spring 1941

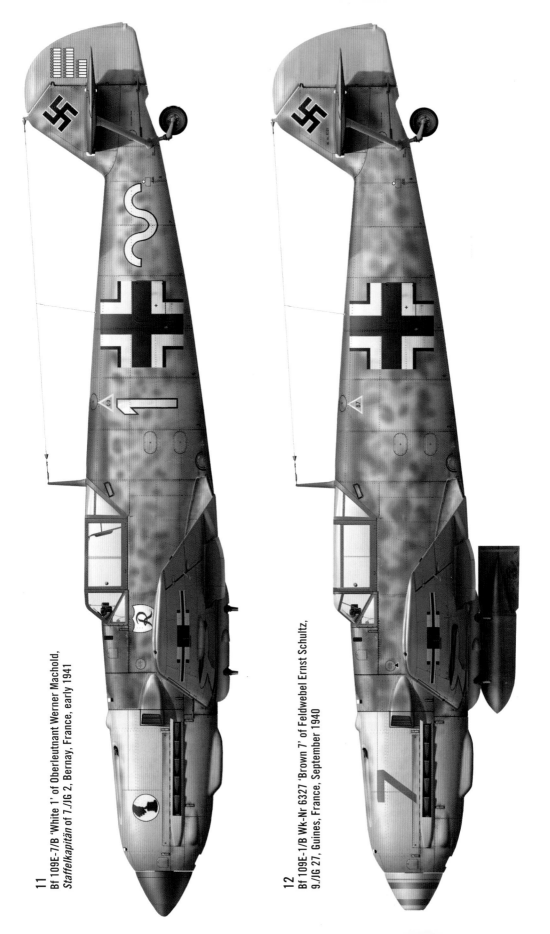

11
Bf 109E-7/B 'White 1' of Oberleutnant Werner Machold,
Staffelkapitän of 7./JG 2, Bernay, France, early 1941

12
Bf 109E-1/B Wk-Nr 6327 'Brown 7' of Feldwebel Ernst Schultz,
9./JG 27, Guines, France, September 1940

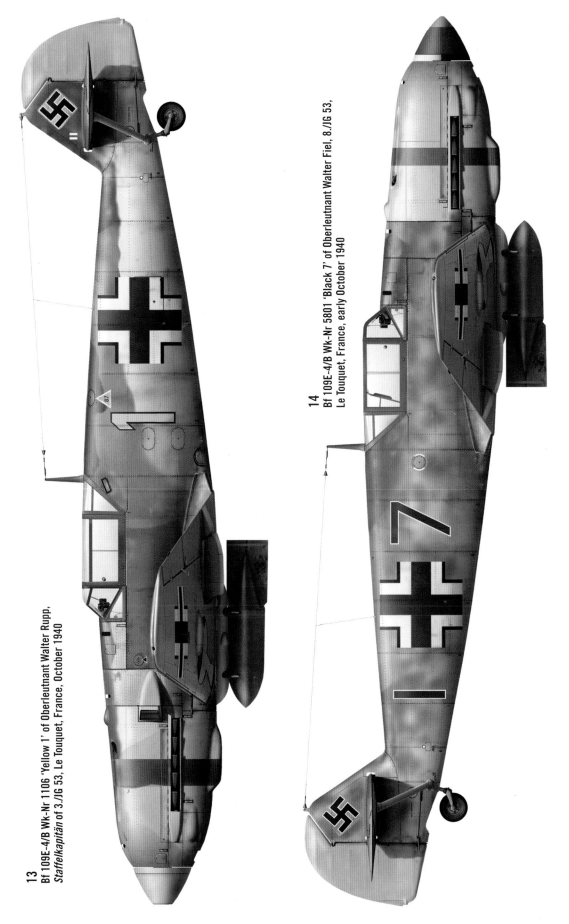

13
Bf 109E-4/B Wk-Nr 1106 'Yellow 1' of Oberleutnant Walter Rupp,
Staffelkapitän of 3./JG 53, Le Touquet, France, October 1940

14
Bf 109E-4/B Wk-Nr 5801 'Black 7' of Oberleutnant Walter Fiel, 8./JG 53,
Le Touquet, France, early October 1940

15
Bf 109F-4/B Wk-Nr 7629 'Blue 1' + 'Chevron and Bar' of Oberleutnant Frank Liesendahl,
Staffelkapitän of 10.(*Jabo*)/JG 2, Beaumont-le-Roger, France, May–June 1942

16
Bf 109F-4/B 'Blue 7' + 'Chevron and Bar' of 10.(*Jabo*)/JG 2,
Beaumont-le-Roger, France, May 1942

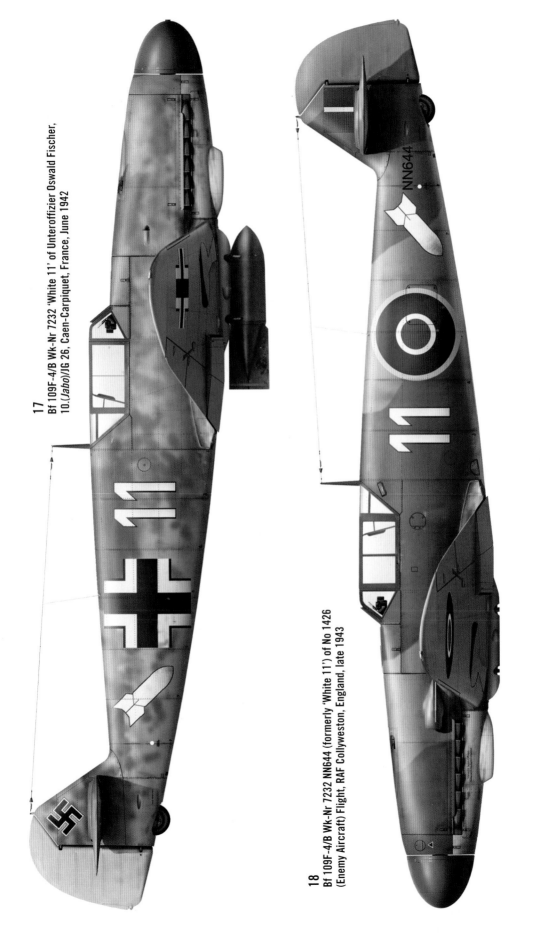

17
Bf 109F-4/B Wk-Nr 7232 'White 11' of Unteroffizier Oswald Fischer, 10.(*Jabo*)/JG 26, Caen-Carpiquet, France, June 1942

18
Bf 109F-4/B Wk-Nr 7232 NN644 (formerly 'White 11') of No 1426 (Enemy Aircraft) Flight, RAF Collyweston, England, late 1943

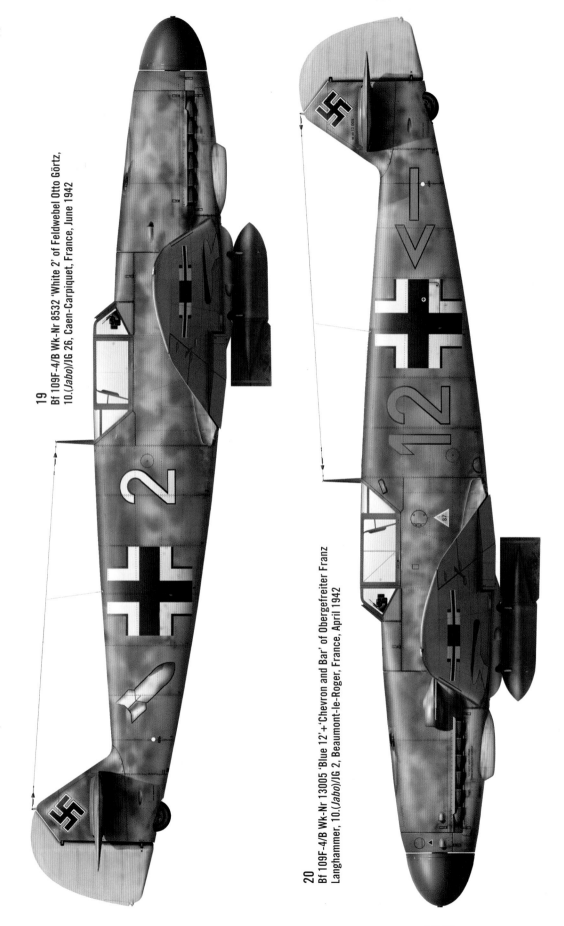

42

19
Bf 109F-4/B Wk-Nr 8532 'White 2' of Feldwebel Otto Görtz,
10.(Jabo)/JG 26, Caen-Carpiquet, France, June 1942

20
Bf 109F-4/B Wk-Nr 13005 'Blue 12' + 'Chevron and Bar' of Obergefreiter Franz
Langhammer, 10.(Jabo)/JG 2, Beaumont-le-Roger, France, April 1942

21
Bf 109G-14 Wk-Nr 781183 'Blue 3' of Unteroffizier Werner Zetzschke, 4./JG 4, Darmstadt-Griesheim, Germany, 1 January 1945

22
Bf 109G-14/AS Wk-Nr 784986 'Yellow 19' of Oberfeldwebel Paul Schwerdtfeger, 11./JG 6, Bissel, Germany, 1 January 1945

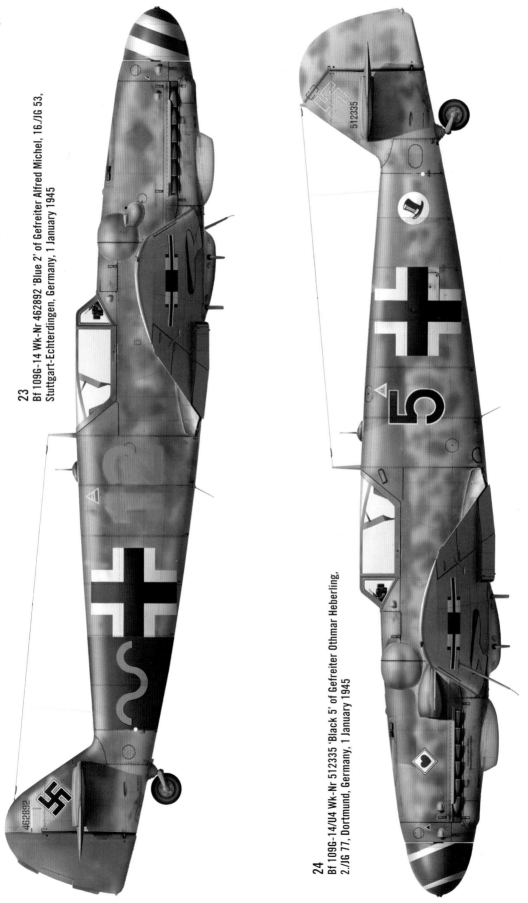

23
Bf 109G-14 Wk-Nr 462892 'Blue 2' of Gefreiter Alfred Michel, 16./JG 53, Stuttgart-Echterdingen, Germany, 1 January 1945

24
Bf 109G-14/U4 Wk-Nr 512335 'Black 5' of Gefreiter Othmar Heberling, 2./JG 77, Dortmund, Germany, 1 January 1945

CHAPTER THREE

NEW CHALLENGES

Oberfeldwebel Gerhard Limberg of 10.(*Jabo*)/JG 2 confers with Leutnant Leopold Wenger (back to camera) and a shirtless groundcrewman at an airfield in France – probably Caen-Carpiquet – in the early summer of 1942. Behind them is Bf 109F-4/B 'Blue 2', complete with a hand crank sticking out of the starboard side of the engine compartment (*Chris Goss Collection*)

By the end of 1940, it was clear that any possibility of an invasion of Britain was becoming less and less likely. The Battle of Britain had decisively ended that intention for the time being, and during the early months of 1941 the emphasis of German strategy was irrevocably turning towards the Soviet Union. The gradual run-down of Luftwaffe units facing Britain continued well into the opening months of the new year, with more and more *Gruppen* withdrawn back to Germany or to further-flung occupied parts of the Continent.

Nevertheless, the fight still needed to be taken to the British on the Channel Front, with a continuation of the operations of the summer and autumn of 1940, albeit on a considerably reduced scale and with far more limited objectives. Such actions would usefully tie-up RAF resources at a time when the British had successfully started to make fighter sweeps and limited tactical bombing missions of their own against German targets in Occupied Europe. Continuing operations on the Channel Front, even if significantly limited, could also hide, to a certain extent, the movement of Luftwaffe forces away from the West and their concentration elsewhere, principally in the East.

Comparatively limited operations against southern England were flown by several units, some of these being more in the form of 'nuisance' raids rather than actual *Jabo* operations. Named *Störangriff* (harassing attack) and *Tiefangriff* (strafing attack), these were small-scale annoyance attacks usually carried out simply by the conventional fighter *Staffeln* rather than the dedicated *Jabo* units. They could involve the strafing of particular locations or targets of opportunity, and sometimes they were little more than simple armed reconnaissance sorties.

Conversely, these types of attack were also increasingly used by RAF fighters that were progressively operating in ever-growing numbers over the Continent from 1941 onwards. Later in the war, such mission profiles were utilised by the Allies with considerable effect during and after the D-Day period from June 1944 onwards.

Due to the increasing RAF activity over northern France and the Low Countries in the first half of 1941, the Luftwaffe *Jagdgeschwader* were needed to provide fighter cover in these areas to counter enemy operations. To fulfil this requirement, several Bf 109 units continued to be based in the areas controlled by *Luftflotten* 2 and 3 in northern France. The former included units in the Pas de Calais and surrounding areas such as I. and II.(S)/LG 2 and ErprGr 210, as well as JG 3 and JG 26. Further west, in the areas controlled by *Luftflotte* 3, were JG 2 and parts of JG 77. This requirement meant in practical terms that the fighter *Geschwader* on the Channel Front were now

The leading light of JG 2's *Jabo* effort was Oberleutnant Frank Liesendahl, the successful *Staffelkapitän* of 13./JG 2 (later redesignated 10./JG 2). A veteran of combat in Poland (with II./ZG 1), the *Blitzkrieg* in France and the Battle of Britain, he helped perfect the tactics that were employed by the *Jabo* Bf 109F fighter-bombers on the Channel Front during 1941–42 *(Chris Goss Collection)*

on the defensive, which had not been the case during the Battle of Britain when the Luftwaffe was on the attack.

To that end, several of the *Jabo* units that had formed in the latter part of 1940 continued with this more formal tasking into the early months of 1941. A limited number of more organised attacks against specific high-value targets in southern England were also carried out, mainly involving LG 2.

However, the coming of Germany's major shift in strategic planning from Western Europe to the Soviet Union saw the eventual removal of several units that had been important Bf 109 *Jabo* operators during the Battle of Britain. Amongst them was ErprGr 210, the original instigator of the Bf 109E's fledgling *Jabo* combat activity. This *Gruppe* had persisted with its *Jabo* activities into 1941, principally from Calais-Marck, although it remained headquartered at Denain. However, in April 1941, the unit moved briefly to Abbeville in northeastern France, prior to a major relocation east and an eventual re-designation.

During this time II.(S)/LG 2 also persisted with its *Jabo* activities, albeit on a smaller scale than the larger set-piece attacks that it had participated in during the latter part of the Battle of Britain. Sorties against high-value targets such as airfields were carried out, but these were risky. On

8 February 1941, for example, two Bf 109E-7/Bs attacked the key RAF airfield at Hawkinge. One was downed by the base's anti-aircraft guns and its pilot killed when he unwisely made a second pass across the airfield.

Eventually even LG 2 was no longer involved in *Jabo* operations across the English Channel. During late March 1941, both I.(J)/LG 2 and II.(S)/LG 2 were withdrawn from their long-standing home of Calais-Marck (I. *Gruppe* had been transferred temporarily to Germany in early November 1940, taking up residence at Köln-Butweilerhof, only to return to Calais-Marck just before year-end). Earmarked like other units for operations against the Soviet Union, I. *Gruppe* moved to Wien in Austria, while II. *Gruppe* was transferred to Belitsa-Nord in the Kingdom of Bulgaria, thence to Plovdiv, also in Bulgaria, during April 1941. In similar fashion to several other units that were intended for action against Soviet forces, they were firstly diverted for operations over Greece and Yugoslavia in the Balkans.

The removal of these dedicated *Jabo* units from the Channel Front put the emphasis back onto 'normal' fighter *Geschwader* to fill the gap. In the event, two units became specifically involved in fighter-bomber activity during 1941 against targets in southern England and in the English Channel, eventually using the new Bf 109F-series. JGs 2 and 26 were both 'old timers' in the operational employment of the Bf 109. These fighter *Geschwader* proved to be formidable opponents for the RAF aircraft that were increasingly venturing across the English Channel to draw the Luftwaffe into battle and to attack specific targets. They were also basically alone in providing fighter cover over the Channel Front due to the many other fighter *Geschwader* being gradually but increasingly removed from the West and readied for the coming onslaught against the Soviet Union.

During the early months of 1941, JG 2's *Stab*, I. and II. *Gruppe* had been based at Beaumont-le-Roger, with III. *Gruppe* at Bernay, all within *Luftflotte* 3. JG 26 had been located further east at Abbeville-Drucat as a part of *Luftflotte* 2. Of these bases, the former *Armée de l'Air* aerodrome of Beaumont-le-Roger was well situated, roughly equidistant between the Pas de Calais and the Cherbourg peninsula, and therefore within striking distance of a large swathe of southern England. Similarly, Abbeville and airfields in the Pas-de-Calais were suitably located for action over southeast England and London.

Within JG 2, three *Staffeln* were specifically delegated to *Jabo* operations. Initially, these were JG 2's 2., 6. and 7. *Staffeln*. At that time a fighter *Geschwader* was still comprised of *Gruppen* each with three *Staffeln*, and so these three were each drawn from a different *Gruppe*. Leading 7./JG 2 was the accomplished fighter pilot Oberleutnant Werner Machold. 2. *Staffel* was headed by Oberleutnant Siegfried Bethke, with Oberleutnant Frank Liesendahl in charge of 6./JG 2. Some members of JG 2 had already received training for fighter-bomber operations, Bethke being one of the pilots seconded to ErprGr 210 at Denain for schooling in *Jabo* tactics during November 1940 after the original orders had been issued for *Jagdgeschwader* to convert a number of their *Staffeln* in fighter-bomber units.

With the gradual coming into service of the Bf 109F, *Jabo* operations against southern England became more organised – and deadly. The 'Friedrich' was appeciably more advanced than the 'Emil' that had previously flown all the single-engined conventional fighter and *Jabo* attacks against Britain. The F-model was a logical development of the 'Emil', and represented a step forward for the basic Bf 109 layout and mission capability. It drew on many of the lessons learned from the development of the Bf 109E into a longer-range fighter-bomber. Indeed, some pilots felt that the 'Friedrich' was the best of all Bf 109 versions. But it also had its critics. These included Adolf Galland, who felt the type was under-gunned due to the removal of the wing cannon of the later marks of Bf 109E.

Design work on an improved 'Emil' had been in hand at Messerschmitt for many months before the 'Friedrich' gained operational status with the Luftwaffe. One of the improvements that Robert Lusser, Willy Messerschmitt and the other designers and aerodynamicists at the Bayerische Flugzeugwerke had intended to perfect for the Bf 109F when work initially began on this new Bf 109 version was – at last – the 'engine-mounted' cannon installation to fire through the propeller spinner. This was achieved with the 'F-series, a 20 mm MG FF or more usually MG FF/M cannon being centrally positioned in an installation that was successful and was widely used thereafter, although the weapon type was soon changed.

Aerodynamically, the new Bf 109F was a cleaner design than the 'Emil' that preceded it. This gave the 'Friedrich' better performance for its primary fighter mission, but it also played an important part in the type's adoption for the *Jabo* role.

Although powered by the same DB 601N engine as fitted in the late Bf 109E-series, including the E-7, the 'Friedrich' emerged with a more streamlined engine cowling shape and a smoothly rounded spinner. The bracing below the horizontal tailplane of the 'Emil' was deleted and the wing shape was revised, with rounded wingtips being the most obvious manifestation of this revision. The wing flaps were also completely redesigned and the tailwheel was made partly retractable.

However, the wing cannon of the later 'Emils' were deleted, leaving the Bf 109F armed with two standard MG 17 7.92 mm machine guns in the upper forward fuselage and the new centrally mounted 20 mm cannon firing through the spinner. This occasioned Adolf Galland to have two F-series airframes specially converted with greater firepower, although his ideas about increasing the calibre and extent of weaponry for the 'Friedrich' were not taken up.

Writing messages on bombs was a past-time that appears to have been followed by airmen and groundcrews amongst all the major combatants of World War 2. The likelihood of anyone reading the message was zero, unless the bomb failed to explode and needed to be inactivated. In this rare colour image, a Bf 109F from 10. (*Jabo*) of either JG 2 or JG 26 provides the backdrop for a 250-kg SC 250 bomb as the weapon receives its 'artwork' from an Unteroffizier prior to the aircraft's next sortie (*EN Archive*)

Following several crashes by early Bf 109Fs, it was found necessary to add strengthening to the rear fuselage in the form of two external stiffeners on either side beneath the horizontal tail. However, in the same area, the external rudder control linkage of the 'Emil' was replaced by an internal arrangement that also added to the Bf 109F's greater airframe tidiness and streamlining.

Production of the F-series was initially entrusted to Wiener Neustädter Flugzeugwerke (WNF) in Austria and to Messerschmitt's Regensburg plant. The manufacturing of operational examples began with the Bf 109F-1, which was produced in limited numbers. A production plan published by the *Reichsluftfahrtministerium* (RLM – German Ministry of Aviation) in October 1940 described the projected construction of the early examples of the F-series, which had been intended to commence during July 1940. A total of 208 Bf 109F-1s are known to have been built.

The first operational recipient of the F-1 was JG 51 on the Channel Front, which was fully committed to fighter and fighter-bomber operations during the Battle of Britain. An early example was assigned to the *Stab* of JG 51 for *Geschwaderkommodore* Major Werner Mölders, who initially used the aircraft in aerial combat during October 1940. It was thanks primarily to JG 51 that the 'Friedrich' was given a good operational 'shake down', although at that time this did not involve *Jabo* missions. In addition to *Stab*/JG 51, the *Geschwader*'s I. *Gruppe* also began receiving examples during November 1940 to partially re-equip with the type, although the unit's 'Emils' continued to persist.

The Bf 109F-2 was the first major production model of the F-series. The engine for initial examples was the DB 601N, but with slightly wider propeller blades. A revised, rounded and more prominent supercharger air intake was fitted to the port side of the engine cowling.

Significantly, the F-series introduced a cut-off valve for the coolant radiators under the wings. These were susceptible to ground fire, and the resulting loss of coolant if hit would lead to potential seizure of the engine. But with the valves installed, a holed radiator could now be isolated before the coolant drained out of the system. The cut-off valves were, therefore, a potentially life-saving solution, but for unknown reasons they were only fitted to a comparatively small number of airframes. The relevant valves were not installed in the factory, but came as a kit for 'in the field' installation at unit level. Clearly, these were useful add-ons for Bf 109Fs conducting *Jabo* operations at low-level, where the danger of ground fire knocking out the cooling system was obviously great.

The installation of armoured glass to the centre windscreen was also an important safety feature for the F-series. Again, this was a significant fitment for Bf 109Fs engaging in *Jabo* operations.

The F-2 had a slightly different armament arrangement to the initial F-1, the centrally mounted MG FF/M being replaced by a 15 mm MG 151/15 cannon, apparently as an interim measure. Provision was also built into the type on the production line to allow it to carry a 300-litre drop tank beneath the fuselage – an external store that was by then of great significance. A comparatively small number of F-2s were fitted with bomb racks in the same location for either one 250-kg or four 50-kg bombs. When installed, these precluded the use of the external fuel tank. The exact number of fighter-bomber F-2s built remains unknown, but the designation Bf 109F-2/B appears to have been assigned to these aircraft.

In total, some 1380 F-2s were eventually constructed by Messerschmitt at Regensburg, WNF, Erla, Arado and AGO Flugzeugwerke. Production was principally between October 1940 and August 1941, with initial examples reaching operational Luftwaffe units during the new year of 1941.

The F-2 was followed by the second major production model of the 'Friedrich' series, the Bf 109F-4, and it was this version that included *Jabo* variations that were so important – if comparatively briefly – to the fighter-bomber campaign in the West. Unlike the preceding 'Friedrich' versions, the F-4 was powered by the more powerful DB 601E engine of some 1350 hp for take-off. Although offering greater output, this powerplant could be run on the more commonly available 87 Octane fuel, rather than the 96–100 Octane C3 required by the DB 601N.

The Bf 109F-4 included revised armament, the centrally mounted MG 151/15 15 mm cannon of the F-2 being replaced by a harder-hitting MG 151/20 20 mm weapon. The upper forward fuselage MG 17 machine guns remained unaltered. It is believed that some 1841 Bf 109F-4s were built by the same manufacturers as the F-2, excluding AGO, which was involved in other programmes including starting to prepare for Fw 190 production.

The 300-litre drop tank carried under the fuselage was a standard installation for all F-2s and F-4s with the necessary plumbing in place. For the Bf 109F-4, a certain number were configured to be fitted with an underfuselage bomb rack like the F-2 for either one 250-kg or four 50-kg bombs as genuine *Jabo* 'Friedrich' variants. All the necessary electrics and plumbing were included on the production line. This gave rise to the Bf 109F-4/B, which was more numerous than the Bf 109F-2/B. Initial examples of the F-4 reached frontline units in June 1941.

'Blue 7' was a Bf 109F-4/B assigned to 13.(*Jabo*)/JG 2 in 1941–42. This unit was re-designated 10.(*Jabo*)/JG 2 in April 1942, but retained the blue numbers as befitted a 13th *Staffel*. Interestingly, this aircraft featured a scoreboard of shipping attacks on its rudder similar to that of Oberleutnant Frank Liesendahl's famous 'Blue 1', suggesting either that several aircraft in the *Staffel* had the same rudder markings showing the achievements of the entire unit, or this aircraft was later re-numbered as 'Blue 1' (*EN Archive*)

FRONTLINE EXCELLENCE

In service, the *Jabo* Bf 109Fs proved ideal for continuing and extending the work already carried out by the 'Emil' fighter-bombers during the Battle of Britain and subsequent months. The fight still needed to be taken to the British on the Channel Front, and the new Bf 109F-series was the ideal type with which to continue these operations in the summer and autumn of 1941. And so began a new phase of organised *Jabo* attacks against targets in southern England, sometimes referred to as 'tip and run' sorties, although they have also been called 'hit and run' raids.

A significant amount of the work that was carried out to develop and perfect these attacks was undertaken by Oberleutnant Frank Liesendahl. In the same way that Werner Mölders was responsible for developing important concepts of aerial warfare, including the four-aircraft *Schwarm* used so successfully by *Jagdwaffe* units during the *Blitzkrieg* period, so Liesendahl created concepts and methods of attack that were suited to the Bf 109 *Jabo*s. And in keeping with Mölders' *Schwarm* formations, Liesendahl's concepts were based around the basic four-aircraft arrangement.

Unfortunately, definite details of Liesendahl's Luftwaffe career are scarce. It is believed that he participated in the campaign against Poland in September 1939 while flying with II./ZG 1. In mid-November 1939 he was posted to JG 2 – the unit with which he duly flew all his subsequent operations. With the rank of Oberleutnant, Liesendahl was *Gruppenadjutant* of II./JG 2 during the Battle of France. This *Gruppe* began the French campaign at Nordholz, but it soon moved across northern France as the German army (*Heer*) captured French airfields. The *Gruppe* was at Evreux when the Battle of France ended, after which it moved to Beaumont-le-Roger.

Liesendahl had had a lucky escape during the Dunkirk battle. Having been shot down and wounded while ground strafing on 26 May, he was quickly captured. However, during that period, German PoWs were rarely transported to Britain because vessels were overloaded with British and French troops seeking to flee Dunkirk. Liesendahl was therefore released when German forces freed him. This would prove to be a costly blow for the Allies. Fully recovered from his injuries, he subsequently took command of 6./JG 2 just as all *Jagdgeschwader* were expected to re-purpose several of their *Staffeln* into *Jabo* units.

Some sources have claimed that Liesendahl was an accomplished fighter pilot in aerial combat with a number of victories, but there is no evidence that he was credited with a single aerial success. On the contrary, he thrived in air-to-ground operations.

Although Liesendahl was obviously an enthusiast for *Jabo* operations, there was generally little enthusiasm within both JG 2 and JG 26 to perform these dangerous missions which were subsequently carried out in a rather piecemeal fashion. Indeed, it appears that the *Jabo Staffeln* of JG 2 flew conventional fighter sorties very often, with the *Jabo* mission considered (at least at unit level) to be a distant second in priority. It is true that JG 2 did not in fact fly *Jabo* sorties at all in 1940, only taking up this operational requirement during 1941. Oberleutnant Werner Machold, the *Staffelkapitän* of 7./JG 2, was hardly an enthusiast for fighter-bomber missions, being a successful pilot in aerial combat.

When *Jabo* attacks were flown by the less than impressed JG 2 pilots, they were sometimes unsuccessful. The mission on 26 April 1941 appears to have been an

Three *Staffeln* within JG 2 were converted to operate *Jabo* Bf 109Es and flew operations during 1941. One of them was 7./JG 2, led by the charismatic ace Oberleutnant Werner Machold. First and foremost a fighter pilot, he preferred aerial combat, but nonetheless flew a number of *Jabo* sorties. On 9 June 1941, at the controls of Bf 109E-7/Z Wk-Nr 5983 'White 15', Machold was forced to crash land near Swanage after his aircraft was hit by anti-aircraft fire from a Royal Navy destroyer during a low-level *Jabo* attack on a convoy off Portland. Following his capture, Machold told his interrogator that 'this was the first time he had carried out a bombing attack on shipping, and he had previously resisted the prostitution of his art as a fighter pilot'! (*Malcolm V Lowe Collection*)

early, if not the first, such operation by 2./JG 2. The intention was to strike at shipping off the major port of Portsmouth, in Hampshire, but was not a success. On 11 May the significant RAF airfield of Warmwell in Dorset was the intended target, but the *Staffel*-strength attack was a total failure. The Messerschmitt pilots failed to locate the airfield, and instead attacked targets of opportunity along the nearby coastline.

Several further anti-shipping attacks were also made, with questionable success, although Liesendahl himself was credited with inflicting damage on a cargo ship off Shoreham, on the West Sussex

The forward fuselage and nose of one of the Bf 109F *Jabos* of 10.(*Jabo*)/JG 2, showing the location of the *Staffel's* insignia – a dark red fox with a broken cargo ship in its mouth. This marking was allegedly designed by Oberleutnant Frank Liesendahl's fiancée. (*EN Archive*)

coast. Oberleutnant Bethke led an attack by a *Schwarm* from 2./JG 2 against vessels in Swanage Bay on 14 May. Five days later, the attacking Messerschmitts were met by Spitfires from No 234 Sqn based at Warmwell. The target was a coastal convoy off Portland, in Dorset, which survived unscathed according to available British records. Two of the Bf 109s were lost (they were apparently from 1./JG 2, flying a post-strike reconnaissance mission), while Machold was credited with downing two Spitfires (claims that tally exactly with No 234 Sqn's losses that day).

Although the final *Jabo* mission by 2./JG 2 was flown on 30 May against Portland itself, Machold's 7./JG 2 continued to perform fighter-bomber sorties after that date. However, on 9 June, Machold himself was shot down while flying Bf 109E-7/Z Wk-Nr 5983 'White 15'. At that time not all of JG 2 had converted to the 'Friedrich' – the Bf 109E-7/Z was an uprated version of the E-7 with a GM-1 nitrous oxide injection system to boost the engine's performance for short periods during combat, especially at higher altitudes. Machold force landed near Swanage and was captured after having been hit by anti-aircraft fire from a Royal Navy destroyer while making a low-level *Jabo* attack on a convoy off Portland. By that time he had been credited with 32 aerial victories in more than 250 combat sorties.

Clearly, these attacks were not a success in terms of overall destruction, and it appears that the three *Jabo Staffeln* of JG 2 subsequently reverted to conventional fighter activities. However, their *Jabo* operations did have the positive effect for the Germans of tying-up British defences. It was clear that something more substantial was needed. Shot down again, this time in July 1941, Liesendahl was out of combat for some time. However, upon his return to JG 2, he enthusiastically argued for the creation within both JGs 2 and 26 of properly dedicated *Jabo* units. These two *Jagdgeschwader* were still the only fighter units on the Channel Front.

By then, JG 2 was led by Major Walter Oesau, who seemingly had a good working relationship with Liesendahl. The result was the establishment of new, dedicated *Jabo Staffel* 13./JG 2 on 10 November

Typical of the merchant shipping that Oberleutnant Liesendahl's *Jabo* pilots specialised in attacking was SS *Lieutenant Robert Mory*, a 3000-ton French-owned cargo steamship that was bombed on 10 February 1942. Although such attacks were sometimes successful, there were never enough Bf 109F *Jabos* to make a telling difference to the course of the war (*Malcolm V Lowe Collection*)

1941 at Beaumont-le-Roger. During that time it was unusual for fighter *Geschwader* to have an operational 13th *Staffel*, and for paperwork purposes the new squadron was delegated to JG 2's II. *Gruppe*. It is not known if the commanding officer of II./JG 2, Hauptmann Karl-Heinz Greisert, was enamoured with having a *Jabo Staffel* within his command, and in the event 13./JG 2 acted largely independently under Liesendahl's leadership.

To begin with, the unit embarked on a long training period in which Liesendahl's fighter-bomber theories were defined and training was undertaken. Some of the pilots who had flown in JG 2's previous *Jabo Staffeln* joined the new unit.

Although still technically not yet declared operational, 13./JG 2 undertook several *Jabo* sorties in late 1941 and early 1942. The first of these appears to have been on 25 December 1941 against Fairlight, in East Sussex. However, Liesendahl emphasised attacks on shipping as much as against targets on land. This inevitably included merchant vessels, which Liesendahl had already sought out in previous attacks.

On 10 February 1942, 13./JG 2 put up a major effort against shipping along the Cornish coast. During this mission, the French-owned 3000-ton steamship SS *Lieutenant Robert Mory* of the Mory et Cie. company previously based in Boulogne was bombed and badly damaged. For his bravery that day, *Robert Mory*'s Chief Engineer Bert Bateman of the Merchant Navy was awarded the MBE.

13./JG 2 was, technically, still non-operational when this operation took place, its pilots being drilled in how to perform what would turn out to be its most effective method of attack. This was known as the Liesendahl Verfahren ('Liesendahl Method'). It involved a very fast initial low-level approach at virtually wave-top or tree-top height at a speed of around 450 km/h. When 1800 m from the intended target, the pilot would effect a rapid climb to an altitude of 500 m before levelling off. A dive towards the target was then made at a preferred angle of three degrees, with airspeed increasing to around 550 km/h. Using the aircraft's Revi gunsight, the pilot would then pull up and release the 250-kg bomb beneath the fuselage. By so doing, he effectively lobbed the bomb towards the target. With considerable practice, this method of attack could be made to be very accurate and effective.

Liesendahl's *Staffel* officially became operational on 18 February 1942, equipped with fighter-bomber Bf 109Fs. It generated sorties as soon as the weather permitted, having been given responsibility for attacking targets in the western Channel area of southwest England. Up to that point, there had been a lull in significant fighter-bomber activity over southern England for several months, but the coming into service of 13./JG 2 rapidly changed that situation.

Several operations took place during March, the first of these seemingly being on the 7th when four Bf 109Fs evaded radar detection by flying very low over the English Channel until they made landfall near Exmouth, Devon. They then spent several minutes machine-gunning anything and everything in the Exmouth and Teignmouth areas, without any particular regard to singling out worthwhile military targets. An attempt was made to intercept the raiders by Polish-manned No 317 Sqn from RAF Bolt Head but without success. The response to this and subsequent missions illustrated the problem of countering such small, low-altitude fast-moving raids. It was virtually impossible for radar to detect this type of mission profile, and the only real answer in the long-term was for the RAF to mount standing patrols of fighters that were ready to intercept incoming raids – and these attempts were not by any means always successful.

DESTRUCTIVE RAIDS

For the time being, Liesendahl's *Jabos* were able to wreak havoc on the coastal towns of Devon. Small local convoys and harbour installations became a familiar set of targets, with Torquay and Brixham being particularly hard hit. On 31 March the unit achieved a major success by sinking a 3000-ton collier off Brixham. Led by Liesendahl, who shared in the destruction of the ship with Leutnant Erhard Nippa, the four-aircraft *Schwarm* again approached their target undetected. But this time the shore defences were alert and fatally damaged the Messerschmitt of Unteroffizier Gottfried Weiser, who bailed out of his stricken *Jabo* near the Channel Islands – his body was never recovered.

At the start of April, 13./JG 2 was re-designated 10./JG 2 (or, to give it the full title, 10.(*Jabo*)/JG 2). That month saw a considerable expansion in *Jabo*

The rudder of Bf 109F-4/B Wk-Nr 7629 'Blue 1', the well-known aircraft of Oberleutnant Frank Liesendahl. The *Staffelkapitän* of 13.(*Jabo*)/JG 2 (later 10.(*Jabo*)/JG 2), Liesendahl had the tail adorned with the silhouettes of vessels that had been attacked and the successes claimed during anti-shipping operations. Six such markings, blacked in to show hits or complete sinking claims, were visible at the time this photograph was taken (*Tony Holmes Collection*)

Oberleutnant Liesendahl studies the rudder of his Bf 109F-4/B Wk-Nr 7629 'Blue 1' at Beaumont-le-Roger in early June 1942. By then 13.(*Jabo*)/JG 2 had been re-designated 10.(*Jabo*)/JG 2, and eight ship silhouettes now adorned the yellow rudder, the most recent being dated 7 June 1942. During the course of that month the unit began transitioning onto the more potent and powerful Fw 190A *Jabo* (*Chris Goss Collection*)

attacks, British intelligence sources assuming that more than 150 such raids were the work of the small force of fighter-bombers. The established sorties against coastal targets were added to by bolder missions against specific high-value locations further inland. These included highly prominent gas holders, which were easy to find, but just about anything was the target of the Messerschmitt pilots' machine gun and cannon fire. Included were houses as well as obvious military targets, giving much frustration to the British defenders who were finding it very difficult to counter these attacks.

Missions often included just a four-aircraft *Schwarm*, marking them out as totally different to the large *Jabo* attacks of the later Battle of Britain period during October 1940. JG 2's *Jabo* pilots came to know the western Channel very well, where prominent landmarks and the distinctive shape of the coastline made finding specific targets easy after a fast incoming dash across the water at low-level.

Liesendahl's usual mount was Bf 109F-4/B Wk-Nr 7629 'Blue 1'. It bore the distinctive squadron markings of a blue chevron and horizontal bar behind the fuselage cross, and the *Staffel* emblem of a dark red fox with a ship in its mouth on the port cowling. This insignia is alleged to have been designed by Liesendahl's fiancée. The rudder of this aircraft was decorated with illustrations of ships that presumably referred to sinkings, or hits on particular areas of a target. Eventually eight such side-views were painted on the rudder's port side. It is not confirmed if these were Liesendahl's personal kills or those of the whole unit, it being possible that other aircraft in the *Staffel* also bore similar markings.

An installation of great importance to the *Jabos* of 10./JG 2 was a location of vital significance to Britain's war effort. This was the Telecommunications Research Establishment (TRE) west of Worth Matravers in Dorset, which, amongst other tasks, was heavily involved in radar research. Moved to this location from Dundee in late May and early June 1940 under a different name, the Dorset site proved to be a little too dangerous for the TRE, especially as its location was near to the coastal town of Swanage, with its prominent Swanage Bay and the nearby Old Harry Rocks. These were highly visible local landmarks which could be used by incoming *Jabos* for reference.

Two raids were mounted by 10./JG 2 against the TRE, on 6 and 8 April. Fortunately, the damage caused was nowhere near enough to destroy the site, but two personnel were killed. A hasty decision was made to

relocate the TRE as soon as possible, and in May the establishment moved north to Malvern in Worcestershire, taking up residence in the buildings of Malvern College. It was also feared that the Germans were planning a commando raid on the Dorset site in the wake of Operation *Biting*. This was the famous Bruneval Raid on the night of 27–28 February 1942, when British commandos had captured a German Würzburg radar system from the Bruneval site in northern France. Obviously, the TRE at its exposed Dorset location was a potential target not just for *Jabo* attacks but for a daring commando raid as well, hence its very hasty move north.

Defence against incoming raids by the *Jabo* Messerschmitts continued to be a major headache for the British as the campaign continued. RAF fighters just could not be scrambled quickly enough to intervene, and actually finding the fast, low-flying *Jabos* was in any case a major challenge even if defending aircraft could be vectored into the right areas. Ground- and ship-based anti-aircraft weaponry (especially 40 mm rapid-firing Bofors guns) proved to be of greatest use in meeting the marauding Bf 109s.

As the *Jabo* campaign continued during April and into May 1942, anti-shipping strikes were increasingly successful. These maritime targets tended to be less well-defended than shore installations, and the 'Liesendahl Method' of toss-bombing was much better suited to this type of objective. *Jabo* pilots had found that land targets tended to be surrounded by numerous distractions. Nevertheless, although attacks against shipping continued to mount, these resulted in comparatively small-scale successes, and did not involve the sinking of large merchant vessels or major warships. On 15 May, for example, a fishing boat was sunk in Brixham Harbour and

A scene that was repeated all too frequently during 1942, showing in this case the damage to St Barnabas Vicarage at Bexhill, in East Sussex, on 9 May 1942. *Jabo* attacks unfortunately often resulted in casualties and damage to civilian property that had no military value. Countering these fast-moving, low-level attacks proved to be a headache for British defences (*Andy Saunders Collection*)

Bf 109F-4/B 'White 9' of 10.(*Jabo*)/JG 26 commences its take-off run probably at Caen-Carpiquet, the aircraft's SC 250 bomb virtually scraping the ground as the Messerschmitt accelerates across the grass airfield. This unit was a late-comer to *Jabo* operations in the West, and in the event was one of only two to fly Bf 109F fighter-bombers cross-Channel against English targets, doing so during 1942 (*Chris Goss Collection*)

two others damaged. This was hardly war-winning success, although such an attack showed that the *Jabos* were continuing to foil the British defences.

It was not only the RAF and the anti-aircraft gunners who were frustrated by these attacks. The official Royal Observer Corps history, written after the war ended, pointed out '[Due to] the persistent attacks made by the enemy using very low flying aircraft on coastal targets along the south coast of England, various methods were tried to try to facilitate interception. The difficulties were great as, in view of the low altitude, RDF [radar] information was seriously limited, with the result that anti-aircraft defences were frequently unable to come into action until the attack had been delivered'.

On 16 May, 10./JG 2 went after 'bigger fish' and had a bad day. A six-aircraft raid was made against the very well-defended major port of Plymouth in Devon. Genuine warships were attacked in Plymouth Sound, including the Hunt-class destroyer HMS *Cleveland* (L46), whose anti-aircraft gunners shot down one of the Messerschmitts. Leutnant Hans-Joachim Schulz was killed, and he was subsequently buried with full military honours by the British.

By then, both 10./JG 2 and 10./JG 26 had been brought together under the direction of *Luftflotte* 3. The latter's story was somewhat different to that of Liesendahl's *Staffel*.

JG 26, then under the command of Major Gerhard Schöpfel, was ordered to form its own dedicated *Jabo Staffel* on 10 March 1942 at Saint-Omer-Arques along the same lines as 13./JG 2. This new squadron was designated 10./JG 26 (officially 10.(*Jabo*)/JG 26), and was commanded by Hauptmann Karl Plunser. JG 26's original *Jabo Staffeln*, 3., 4. and 9./JG 26, had been created during the period of autumn/winter 1940 when the *Jagdgeschwader*, participating in the Battle of Britain, had been ordered to convert a fighter *Staffel* within each *Gruppe* into a dedicated *Jabo* unit. This had been performed with little enthusiasm in JG 26, and some of the less disciplined members of the *Geschwader* had been 'lost' by posting them into these generally unwanted *Jabo Staffeln*.

It took some time for the new 10./JG 26 to work-up to any type of operational proficiency at Saint-Omer. There is little evidence that any

help in this respect was forthcoming from Liesendahl's *Staffel*. Nevertheless the unit began operations during April 1942, tasked with covering the southeast of England. On the 24th of that month, Folkestone was attacked by 10./JG 26 in a successful strike that left a gas holder on fire. One person was recorded as killed on the ground, but the attacking Messerschmitts also suffered a loss when Feldwebel Hans-Jürgen Fröhlich was shot down and killed by anti-aircraft fire.

Like the Bf 109Fs of 10./JG 2, the Bf 109F *Jabos* of 10./JG 26 also bore a distinctive marking in the form of a bomb dropping towards its target. This was painted on the rear fuselage behind the cross. The appearance of the design differed from one aircraft to the next, some being heavily shaded, others less so.

One of 10./JG 26's Bf 109F-4/B *Jabos* became something of a celebrity following its last sortie. Built by WNF in 1941 with the Wk-Nr 7232, the aircraft was assigned to 10./JG 26, where it was allocated the number

Close-up detail of the falling bomb symbol of 10.(*Jabo*)/JG 26 that adorned the rear fuselages of its *Jabo* Bf 109Fs in 1942. This particular aircraft, Wk-Nr 8352, was originally built as a Bf 109F-4 by Erla Maschinenwerk at Leipzig and then converted into *Jabo* configuration. The two rear fuselage stiffeners beneath the horizontal tail, characteristic of Bf 109F-series Messerschmitts, are clearly visible in this view (*Chris Goss Collection*)

Bf 109F-4/B Wk-Nr 7232 'White 11' was made airworthy following its belly landing at Beachy Head in May 1942, whereupon it was allocated the serial NN644. Repainted in RAF camouflage and wearing British markings, but retaining its 'White 11' and falling bomb insignia, it joined No 1426 (Enemy Aircraft) Flight and toured airfields, allowing RAF and USAAF personnel to see the enemy up close. The fighter-bomber is seen here with a B-17F Flying Fortress during a visit to RAF Kimbolton, then in Huntingdonshire, home of the USAAF's 379th Bomb Group (*Malcolm V Lowe Collection*)

LEFT
Bf 109F-4/B Wk-Nr 7232 'White 11' flown by Unteroffizier Oswald Fischer of 10./JG 26 following its unscheduled force landing at Beachy Head on 20 May 1942. The pilot very neatly belly landed the aircraft with such care that it was possible for it to be made flyable, although he did shoot at its engine with his pistol following his hasty arrival (*Andy Saunders Collection*)

'White 11'. On 20 May, Unteroffizier Oswald Fischer was part of a two-aircraft *Rotte* attack intended to hit shipping off the East Sussex coast. He later explained what happened during the mission;

'I planned a raid to Brighton since we had not visited the area for some time. Few wanted to fly there because of the long stretch over water. I planned to go inland about 20 miles before we hit the harbour. All worked out fine – a low flight over the Channel and hedgehopping over the British countryside – and right into the harbour at Brighton[sic.] I saw a large ship and told my wingman, "Let's hit it hard!"

'The flak sprayed like a firehose, lazy yellow streaks zipping towards us. But we made it and struck the ship with both bombs. As we exited, I got hit. I could hear impacts, but everything seemed okay. As soon as we were over the water my temperature gauge shot up and I could smell coolant, so I told my wingman to keep low and head towards our base. My engine started to smell very badly, so I turned around and belly landed in a field. I tried to blow the aircraft up, but my explosive charge would not go off. Thus, I became a PoW. I regretted my fate, but it was better than drowning in the English Channel.'

Watched by farm workers at Black Robin Farm on Beachy Head, in East Sussex, Fischer belly landed his Bf 109F-4/B. Having climbed out of the aircraft, he was seen to fire his pistol into the engine in what seemed to the farm labourers to be nothing more than frustrated rage. During his subsequent interrogation, Fischer came up with details which contradicted his later account, as well as making some rather extravagant claims about his war record;

'In the previous month, this pilot made 46 war flights against England when the targets had been Folkestone and Deal railway stations, Hawkinge aerodrome, a colliery near Deal, barracks at Dungeness and some ships off Brighton. One day, he carried out three operations to Folkestone. Other targets included strafing cows, cyclists, buses and railway engines. The pilot claimed 16 victories, three while serving in Libya and 13 over the English Channel. He was the holder of the Iron Cross First Class.'

Historian Andy Saunders looked into Fischer's claims;

'Fischer told his interrogators he started with his wingman from Saint-Omer to attack shipping and harbour installations at Newhaven [seven miles east of Brighton], flying at sea level. No mention was made of penetrating 20 miles inland, but he said that when circling Newhaven, they spotted shipping, including a "corvette", to the southwest of the port and dived to attack. Fischer released his 250-kg bomb towards a "naval vessel", but it struck the water alongside and bounced over it – something contradicted when Oswald Fischer claimed, post-war, that both pilots' bombs had hit their target.'

The 'shipping' which attracted the attention of the pilots was the former River Clyde steamer SS *Davaar*, anchored alongside the entrance channel to Newhaven. 'Kept in steam', it was ready to be swung abeam and sunk as a blockship in the event of invasion. *Davaar* had previously come in for Luftwaffe attention. For example, on 24 March 1942, enemy aircraft attacked and dropped three bombs that narrowly missed it. The vessel's 'in steam' status had doubtless led its attackers to believe the ship was something other than a hulk ready for sacrifice as a defensive measure. All the same, had *Davaar* been hit, it could well have swung about and blocked the port. And with the Dieppe raid (Operation *Jubilee*) due to be launched from Newhaven in August, the sinking of *Davaar* might have had serious consequences.

Fischer had so successfully belly landed his 'White 11' that it was repairable, although a replacement engine had to be found in order for

An excellent in-flight view of Bf 109F-4/B Wk-Nr 7232 'White 11' formerly of 10.(*Jabo*)/JG 26, showing its RAF serial NN644, recently applied Dark Green and Ocean Grey camouflage, yellow undersides and roundels. The aircraft was scrapped post-war (*Tony Holmes Collection*)

Armed with a 250-kg SC 250 bomb beneath its fuselage, Bf 109F-4/B *Jabo* Wk-Nr 8532 'White 2' awaits its next sortie. This photograph was taken at Caen-Carpiquet airfield in the spring of 1942, the aircraft belonging to 10.(*Jabo*)/JG 26. The fighter-bomber was shot down into the sea by anti-aircraft fire while on an evening raid against the Bournemouth area on 6 June 1942, its pilot, Feldwebel Otto Görtz, being killed. Note the additional transparent armoured panel fitted to the aircraft's windscreen for increased pilot protection (*Chris Goss Collection*)

the aircraft to be made flyable again. Airworthy once more, 'White 11' was allocated the British military serial number NN644. Repainted in RAF camouflage and wearing British insignia, but retaining its Luftwaffe 'White 11' and falling bomb markings, the Messerschmitt was placed on the books of No 1426 (Enemy Aircraft) Flight based at RAF Collyweston, in Northamptonshire. It subsequently toured airfields, allowing RAF and USAAF personnel to take a close look at the type of enemy aircraft that they were encountering in aerial combat. 'White 11' continued to be flown in Britain until the aircraft was damaged when it ground looped at Thurleigh, in Bedfordshire. Once repaired, the Bf 109 was passed on to the Enemy Aircraft Flight at RAF Tangmere, in West Sussex, in January 1945 when No 1426 Flight was disbanded. It was subsequently scrapped post-war.

Losses continued for both units. An important success for the British defences was achieved on 27 May when Leutnant Josef Fröschl of 10./JG 2 was shot down while leading a *Schwarm* attack against shipping at Spithead, on the Hampshire coast. By chance, a standing patrol of No 41 Sqn Spitfires based at RAF Merston, a satellite airfield to Tangmere in West Sussex, were watching the Isle of Wight for intruders. This proved to be a successful tactic, as Flt Lt Derek Wainwright succeeded in shooting down Fröschl's Messerschmitt. His combat report stated;

'I was proceeding on patrol to St Catherine's Point [on the Isle of Wight] when I noticed a large column of smoke rising from a ship in the Solent. Almost immediately I saw an Me 109F coming towards me slightly below, followed by a Spitfire. I gave the "Tally ho" and chased it to the starboard side of the Spitfire. After the 109 had dropped its bomb close to a cruiser lying in the mouth of the Solent, he gained speed but soon pulled up in a right hand turn, bringing me into range. I fired a two-second burst, after which it turned away again to port. Soon after that, we again pulled up to starboard in a climbing turn.

'This time I was about 100–200 yards away and practically astern. I gave it a good burst and saw strikes on the fuselage and pieces falling off. He then turned for land and I closed to very close range, overshooting eventually when the pilot bailed out and landed on the Isle of Wight, his aeroplane crashing into a field.'

Fröschl was captured and became a PoW. In his subsequent interrogations, he made a number of unsubstantiated boasts about his combat career, similar to Unteroffizier Fischer, and also sought to mislead his captors with completely incorrect information about the units that he had flown with.

On 9 June, one of 10./JG 26's most able *Jabo* pilots, Oberleutnant Hans Ragotzi, was shot down and killed. Taking part in a raid against East Wittering, in West Sussex, his victor was Plt Off Keith Mason of No 131 Sqn based at RAF Merston.

MAJOR CHANGES

During June 1942, personnel from both 10./JG 2 and 10./JG 26 were gradually relocated from the frontline, although some operations continued. This was done to allow the two dedicated Bf 109 *Jabo Staffeln* to re-equip with the Fw 190, this process principally taking place at Le Bourget airfield in the northeastern suburbs of Paris. The Bf 109F *Jabos* had done a good job with the two *Staffeln* that flew the type up to that point in 1942, and had probably achieved considerably more than their comparatively small numbers would suggest. But the Fw 190 was a completely different, newer and more deadly fighter-bomber.

The first cross-Channel attack with the new Focke-Wulf *Jabos* was undertaken by 10./JG 2 on 7 July. The longer range, faster and more powerful Fw 190A was a major step forward in capability for the *Jabo* pilots, and it was certainly capable of matching anything that the RAF had available to counter it during that period.

Nevertheless, only a short time into the operational use of the *Jabo* Fw 190s, 10./JG 2 suffered a significant loss. After successfully perfecting many of the tactics used by the *Jabos* in the West, and surviving all through the Bf 109 period, Hauptmann Frank Liesendahl was shot down and killed. On 17 July, he was part of a four-aircraft *Schwarm* operating from Caen-Carpiquet. In the proximity of Berry Head near Brixham, the Focke-Wulf pilots attacked the small 1128-ton coastal tanker SS *Daxhound* and its escort of two armed motor launches. The escorts very accurately returned fire, and ML 118 was credited with causing one of the Fw 190s to crash into the sea. Liesendahl's body was discovered in the water off the Devon coast several weeks later.

The arrival of the Fw 190 in the frontline and its gradual integration into the fighter and *Jabo* units on the Channel Front completely transformed the air war in the West. The fast, heavily armed and long-legged Fw 190 gave the Luftwaffe a versatile and potent fighter and fighter-bomber that was a match for the RAF's fighters and ground-based home defences. The Focke-Wulf was also undergoing a development process that saw related versions to the basic Fw 190A fighter in the form of the Fw 190F tactical ground-attack and long-range Fw 190G *Jabo* derivatives enter frontline service.

Oberleutnant Liesendahl is helped with his parachute harness by a member of his groundcrew at Beaumont-le-Roger. Liesendahl became the foremost exponent of the Bf 109F in the *Jabo* role, and led successful missions against southern England, especially shipping in the coastal waters of the English Channel (*Chris Goss Collection*)

Events elsewhere in the world also affected the employment of *Jabo* Bf 109s in the West, initially in a non-operational capacity. On 13 January 1942, a major reorganisation of *Schlacht* units saw the establishment of *Schlachtgeschwader* (SchG or simply SG) 1. This new organisation drew heavily on LG 2, which finally officially ceased to exist at that time. LG 2's fighter component, I.(J)/LG 2 was re-designated I./JG 77. Having been so instrumental in the development of the Bf 109 as a fighter-bomber out of operational necessity during the Battle of Britain period, LG 2's *Schlacht Gruppe* (II.(S)/LG 2) was finally put out to pasture and its personnel posted elsewhere, some to the new *Schlachtgeschwader*. On paper II.(S)/LG 2 became I./SchG 1 on 13 January 1942, with *Stab* II./LG 2 reconfigured as *Stab* I./SchG 1, 4./LG 2 becoming 1./SchG 1, 5./LG 2 re-designated as 2./SchG 1, and 6./LG 2 relaunched as 3./SchG 1.

The *Stab* of this new ground-attack *Gruppe* was based at Werl in the Free State of Prussia (nowadays North Rhine–Westphalia) in the western part of Germany. Leading the unit was *Geschwaderkommodore* Oberstleutnant Otto Weiss, who had formerly led II.(S)/LG 2. Initially, I./SchG 1 was based at Dugino, then from mid-March 1942 at Werl.

The Bf 109 played an important role in this new organisation, providing training for pilots who would soon be flying the aircraft in combat as a fighter-bomber – but not in the West.

A training component of the new *Geschwader* was the unit's *Ergänzungsstaffel* (*Erg.Staffel*/SchG 1), which was formed on 13 January 1942 at Novocherkassk, in the USSR, from *Erg.Staffel* (*Schlacht*)/LG 2.

By then, ErprGr 210 had also ceased to exist in its original form. On 24 April 1941, the unit, with its constituent *Stab* and *Staffeln*, became the components of I. *Gruppe* of new fast attack wing *Schnellkampfgeschwader* (SKG) 210. Although this unit would operate Bf 110s almost exclusively over the Eastern Front following the commencement of Operation *Barbarossa* in June 1941, its *Ergänzungsstaffel* stationed at Merville, in France, had a number of Bf 109Es on its books in addition to its *Zerstörer*.

In this way, the Bf 109 *Jabo* finally disappeared as a frontline aircraft in the West.

CHAPTER FOUR

GRAND FINALE

From 1942 onwards, Bf 109 *Jabos* remained in Luftwaffe service as a major asset in the German war machine. However, the majority of Bf 109 *Jabo* sorties from then on were flown principally over the Eastern Front. Operations were also mounted in the Mediterranean area, specifically over North Africa prior to the Axis capitulation there in May 1943, and later in the defence of Sicily and the Italian mainland.

In the West, the Fw 190 successfully replaced the Bf 109 as the principal *Jabo* type from the summer of 1942 onwards. This allowed the Messerschmitt to be used almost exclusively in its originally intended role as a fighter for aerial combat with enemy aircraft. In that sense from then on the Bf 109 was almost entirely employed as a fighter in the West, and various attempts were made by Messerschmitt to improve the type's operational capabilities in the high-altitude interception role against USAAF heavy bombers that were being increasingly encountered. The Bf 109 in its later versions duly became the mainstay of a Luftwaffe organisation dedicated to attempting to defend the airspace over Occupied Europe and especially over Germany itself under the title *Reichsverteidigung*.

In that role, the Bf 109 in its later versions remained a significant fighter for the Luftwaffe alongside the Fw 190 until the end of the war in Europe on 8 May 1945. However, this did not stem the tide of increasing Allied air superiority in the West. Following the D-Day landings on 6 June 1944, Allied armies inexorably swept forward, liberating France and the Low

A Bf 109G-14 of 12./JG 53 has its DB 605A engine run up at a wintry, wooded Kirrlach airfield in early 1945. More than 5000 G-14s were built from mid-1944 through to war's end, and they were flown by all *Jagdwaffe* units still equipped with Bf 109s at the time of *Bodenplatte*. This aircraft, which has had its undercarriage doors removed, has a three-panel Erla Haube clear-view canopy and a taller fin/rudder – both features of the G-14 (*Tony Holmes Collection*)

Countries and driving on towards Germany itself. The use of air power by the Allies was vitally important to these successes. In particular, Allied fighter-bombers such as the P-47D Thunderbolt and Typhoon – the much more powerful equivalents of the early Bf 109 *Jabos* of 1940–42 – were highly significant.

However, late in the war, in addition to its continuing role of high-altitude fighter, the Bf 109 became involved in operations that saw the type return to 'on the deck' attacks against significant ground targets. A comparative stalemate in the West between Allied and *Heer* forces had developed during the latter weeks of 1944. This gave the Germans the opportunity to plan for a counter-offensive that would potentially be a turning point in their favour. The result was the Ardennes Offensive that began on 16 December 1944, usually referred to in popular culture as the 'Battle of the Bulge', but known to the Germans as '*Wacht am Rhein*' (Watch on the Rhine).

The primary military objective of this substantial ground operation was to deny the enemy further use of the Belgian port of Antwerp, which was highly important to the Allied supply chain. Such a move would split enemy lines, which potentially could have allowed the Germans to encircle and destroy significant elements of the frontline Allied armies.

A key element of the overall operation was to be air power. The Germans were well aware of the importance of owning the skies over the battlefield. This had been successfully exploited initially in Spain during the Spanish Civil War and then in the opening months of World War 2, when the *Blitzkrieg* had been overwhelmingly successful. It was therefore highly important for the Luftwaffe to achieve a significant victory over the Allied air forces in the West as a key element of the planned Ardennes Offensive.

At a meeting of unit commanders convened by Göring in November, the Reichsmarschall made it clear that the Luftwaffe had (in his opinion) been underperforming – yet another example of his often finding fault in those under his command, and blaming those who were not the problem.

With preparations for the planned German ground offensive well progressed, the commanders of various fighter units were called to a conference on 5 December at Flammersfeld near Altenkirchen. It was presided over by Generalmajor Dietrich Peltz, the commander of II. *Jagdkorps*. Here, the first indication of using Luftwaffe fighters – both Bf 109s and Fw 190s – to attack Allied airfields in a mass raid was detailed.

It was intended that the mission would take place during December to coincide with the ground offensive.

This was to be a hammer blow against Allied air strength, and was ultimately named *Unternehmen Bodenplatte* (the word 'Bodenplatte' does not have a direct equivalent meaning in English – it is most often translated as 'Baseplate' or 'Floor Plate', and when freely translated, it can be seen as meaning something like 'the bottom line'). The Germans were fully aware that Allied air power would be able to seriously interfere with the planned ground operation, and so it became the target of the audacious *Bodenplatte* plan.

Although the *Heer*, aided by Waffen-SS units, commenced its ground assault as planned on 16 December, and initially enjoyed considerable surprise and success, critically, the Luftwaffe was mainly grounded due to abysmal weather conditions. The winter of 1944–45 in northwest Europe was one of the harshest of the 20th century, and no operational flying was possible for several days. These inclement atmospheric conditions grounded both the Luftwaffe and Allied air assets.

A limited number of sorties were flown when the bad weather permitted, but the opportunity for the large-scale attack envisaged for *Bodenplatte* was lacking. Ironically, a primary target of the Luftwaffe's *Jabo* aircraft were British and American fighter-bombers, which had already proven their overwhelming value in the Allied advance following D-Day. The RAF and USAAF had learned the lesson from the Luftwaffe that fighter-bombers were now a vital part of combined air and ground operations, as originally pioneered by the Germans several years earlier.

But by late 1944, the Bf 109s in frontline service were very different to the trim 'Emils' and 'Friedrichs' of the earlier war years.

The Bf 109G series had been a follow-on to the F-model, but many seasoned pilots considered it to be a retrograde step. Perpetual weight increase had led to the 'Gustav' being referred to by some pilots as a 'carthorse', while the still comparatively light armament fit in early examples was a continuing cause of consternation at unit level. The G-5 and G-6 introduced more powerful weaponry in the upper forward fuselage position with the adoption of two Rheinmetall-Borsig MG 131 13 mm machine guns in place of the previous MG 17s located there.

In many respects, however, the 'Gustav' series were still competitive with the best of the Allied fighters even in the latter stages of the war when flown by competent and experienced pilots. For the Luftwaffe, such pilots were becoming few and far between due to significant combat attrition by the final months of the war.

The principal Bf 109G versions employed in the *Bodenplatte* attacks were the G-14, G-14/AS and, to a much lesser extent, the K-4. Some Bf 109G-10s are also listed in Luftwaffe records as having taken part.

The most numerous participants were the G-14 and G-14/AS, these variants having entered service during the summer of 1944. Powered by the DB 605A, the Bf 109G-14 was fitted with the MW-50 water/alcohol injection system that allowed the engine extra performance in limited timespans when needed in combat. This was known in production data as the DB 605AM engine, rated at some 1770 hp for take-off. The G-14 also featured as standard the Erla Haube canopy, which had considerably less framing than the structures fitted to earlier marks of Bf 109.

The G-14 and G-14/AS were also an attempt to standardise the 'Gustav' following the long list of sub-types within the major Bf 109G-6 production run. Such narrowing of the design theoretically would also ease the job of construction, which had become highly decentralised due to the successful targeting of industrial areas by Allied bombers up to and including that stage of the war. As a result, few sub-variants were made of the G-14, even though more than 5000 were built, with command fighters and high-altitude variants being the main exceptions.

However, instead of the standard 20 mm MG 151/20 cannon centrally fitted in the engine compartment and firing through the spinner, as successfully pioneered by the 'Friedrich', the Bf 109G-14/U4 sub-type had a 30 mm MK 108 cannon instead. The closely related Bf 109G-14/AS was powered by the DB 605AS engine with an improved, larger supercharger.

It had a more streamlined shape to the forward fuselage that did away with the prominent bumps (*Beule*) ahead of the cockpit that had first appeared on the earlier Bf 109G-5/6 series due to the installation of the MG 131 machine guns. Manufacture was undertaken by the parent company at Regensburg, and by WNF and Erla.

Although the G-14 series represented an attempt at standardisation, in reality there were many variations between production batches from different manufacturers, and even within the same production batch. This was noticeable particularly in the vertical tail shape, some examples having the original small vertical tail as seen on the Bf 109F, while others had a new tall wooden vertical tail, which itself featured several specific design differences. Some examples had a tall tailwheel leg, others retained the earlier, short type.

Much rarer were the Bf 109G-10 and Bf 109K-4. The former came after the G-14, being a part new-build, part conversion series that again attempted to introduce new equipment while trying to establish some continuity into the late-war Bf 109 manufacturing process. In contrast, the K-4 was the last major production model of the whole Bf 109 family. Mainly built by the parent company, although Erla at Leipzig might have constructed some examples, the K-4 was also powered by the same DB 605DM engine as fitted to the G-10, with MW-50 boost increasing power to some 2000 hp on take-off.

These late-war Bf 109s were much more powerful than the earlier marks of the Messerschmitt fighter. Faster than the 'Gustav' series due to aerodynamic refinements that included a retractable tailwheel, the Bf 109K additionally featured more wooden 'non-strategic' major components including the horizontal tailplane surfaces. It was also harder-hitting, having an MK 108 30 mm cannon centrally mounted firing through the propeller spinner. The K-4 began reaching units in the West from mid-October 1944.

None of these late-war Bf 109s were built specifically as *Jabo* models, the Messerschmitt design by that point in the war being intended specifically for aerial combat. This included the need to counter high-flying USAAF heavy bomber raids. Nevertheless, when called on, these late-mark Bf 109s were potentially needed for air-to-ground operations, and this led to their widespread use during the *Bodenplatte* operation. By then, the Luftwaffe was increasingly having to press into service whatever aircraft were available, leading to some types being mis-matched with the tasks that they were delegated.

DELAYED ATTACK

Although the mass attack against Allied airfields had been planned to coincide with the start of the *Heer*'s ground offensive, bad weather continually interrupted these plans. It was therefore not launched until 1 January 1945. By then, the Germans had lost momentum on the ground owing to enemy resistance and clearing weather. The improving climatic conditions allowed Allied aircraft to operate in large numbers against the German ground units, which could not count on successful cover from the Luftwaffe. The *Heer* attempted to regain the initiative by launching Operation *Unternehmen Nordwind* (Northwind). The Luftwaffe was intended to support this new offensive through its *Bodenplatte* attacks on the now revised time schedule.

For *Bodenplatte*, virtually all the fighter units then operational on the Bf 109 would take part, notable exceptions being JGs 51, 300 and 301. The units earmarked for *Bodenplatte* had been diverted from Reich defence fighter duties in the preceding days to help German ground forces wherever possible when weather permitted – mainly by taking on the large numbers of Allied fighter-bombers and medium bombers now airborne looking for targets. But they had also continued with their main tasking of trying to combat US daylight high-altitude heavy bomber raids. This had spread thinly an already depleted fighter force. The once-proud *Jagdwaffe* was now suffering many casualties, forcing it to increasingly rely on inexperienced pilots recently out of training to fill the gaps left by the loss of older more experienced pilots.

The Bf 109-operating units earmarked for *Bodenplatte* were bolstered by *Gruppen* equipped with the Fw 190. By that late stage of the war, several *Jagdgeschwader* were flying both Bf 109s and Fw 190s assigned to specific *Gruppen* within each *Geschwader*. Also incorporated in the *Bodenplatte* plan were to be attacks by jets, but these were not related specifically to the intended sorties of the Bf 109s and Fw 190s.

To aid the different *Gruppen* in finding their allotted targets, 'pathfinder' Junkers Ju 88Gs referred to by the Germans as 'Lotsen' ('guides') were delegated to lead each unit to the vicinity of the specific airfield that it was to attack. These Lotsen Ju 88Gs, drawn from several nightfighter units, were manned by crews adept and experienced in navigation. To avoid detection and not give away their intended target locations until the last minute, each unit was to fly several legs on differing courses during the flight to their assigned airfields, with coloured markers on the ground intended to help with this navigational conundrum.

It was not intended that the Bf 109s or Fw 190s would carry bombs, the objective instead being for them to use their on-board weapons to maximum effect in strafing. This in reality returned the Bf 109 back to its early World War 2 roots when, in the form of impromptu attacks that were carried out during the first months of the war, they used machine gun and cannon fire to destroy ground targets.

Underfuselage drop tanks with additional fuel were essential to allow the Messerschmitts sufficient range to reach their objectives, some of which were almost at the extreme end of what was practicable for the Bf 109s. Obviously the fitment of a fuel tank below the fuselage completely excluded the possibility of carrying a bomb there.

But any form of attack against ground targets, either with bombs or without, was alien to a significant number of the participating Luftwaffe Bf 109 pilots. Veteran fighter pilots and newly arrived airmen alike were not experienced with this form of fighter-bomber operation against a determined and well-armed opponent. Allied intelligence personnel were astonished to learn in the aftermath of the *Bodenplatte* attacks that a significant number of the pilots taking part had very low combat hours – indeed, several were making their first-ever operational flight.

The actual attacks were to be carried out at low-level, the German fighters flying as low as possible all the way to their targets and back –

These smouldering Thunderbolts of the 365th FG's 387th FS were amongst more than 20 P-47Ds destroyed by JG 53 during its strafing attack on Metz-Frescaty (*Malcolm V Lowe Collection*)

around 50 m appears to have been the desired altitude where possible, although some pilots reported being told to approach their targets at 'tree-top' height. Conversely, the *Jagdflieger* were also well aware that Allied light anti-aircraft gun batteries in liberated territory and protecting the airfields themselves were often lethal for low-flying fighters.

The basic formation of the *Schwarm*, as developed by Werner Mölders several years before, and which had been so successful in the *Blitzkrieg* period at the start of World War 2, was still at the centre of Luftwaffe basic formation strategy. However, the *Jagdgeschwader* were somewhat different in structure compared to earlier in the conflict. Each *Gruppe* had been enlarged to contain four *Staffeln*, rather than the three of earlier times. This alteration had been introduced gradually, some *Geschwader* transitioning before others.

The Allied air power that the Luftwaffe intended to take on during *Bodenplatte* was massive. The USAAF's Ninth Air Force and the RAF's 2nd Tactical Air Force (TAF) were numerically much stronger, and had the upper hand by being able to range almost at will over the battlefield. The Allied units were stationed at a variety of airfields in northeastern France and Belgium, plus the comparatively small area of the Netherlands that was in Allied hands. They were all potentially significant targets, but the airfields were well-defended by anti-aircraft batteries. And the Allied fighters occupying these bases were more than capable of looking after themselves in aerial combat with their piston-engined Luftwaffe equivalents. Even fighter-bombers such as the P-47D and Typhoon were potentially deadly adversaries in any dogfight.

The Allied units were also well organised, with the ability to move from one command to another as the situation demanded. Writing after the war, Brig Gen Otto Weyland, head of the Ninth Air Force's XIX Tactical Air Command (TAC), pointed out;

'We shifted groups around from time to time. During the Battle of the Bulge they transferred several groups to my command. I got some from

IX TAC, and even a few from the Eighth Air Force that came over from England. At one time or another, I controlled about 20 groups during the Battle of the Bulge. We had air power running out of our ears. Whenever the weather lifted, the Bulge area became ten-tenths overcast with P-47s, P-51s and P-38s!'

Clearly there were major tactical and operational flaws in the thinking behind *Bodenplatte*, quite apart from the obvious dangers that the attacking force faced from Allied air power and anti-aircraft batteries.

Not all Allied airfields were on the list to be attacked, including those in northeastern France, where Ninth Air Force fighter-bombers were supporting the US Third Army in the Metz-Saar area of operations under XIX TAC control. German intelligence was also short of up-to-date information on several of the potential targets. One of the airfields that was attacked on 1 January, Grimbergen (B60), was devoid of operational flying units, although this appears to have gone unnoticed by the Germans. In other cases, no recent photographic cover was available – the pilots attacking Metz-Frescaty (Y34) had to make do with imagery from when the airfield was previously in German hands.

Above all, surprise was an important element of the operation. The intention was to start the *Bodenplatte* attacks at or around 0920 hrs on 1 January. To that end, the first take-offs were made just before first light, with the Luftwaffe fighters and their pathfinder Ju 88Gs gradually forming up. Being a part of such a large formation was alien to some pilots, although the basic *Schwarm* section of four aircraft flying roughly line abreast was retained. Once the large formations of fighters had formed up, they headed west, shepherded by their pathfinder Ju 88Gs.

The Allies appear to have had little prior specific or detailed knowledge that such a large and coordinated attack was going to take place. A number of unusual Luftwaffe messages had been intercepted by Allied intelligence that suggested some type of tactical operation was planned, but there was no actual detail. However, on several airfields, B-17 and B-24 heavy bombers that had made emergency landings due to battle damage or technical problems were pushed to the centre of the bases to present an ideal, if totally valueless, target for any strafing pilot. This proved to be a very successful plan, as the subsequent events of 1 January were to illustrate.

Although, therefore, not forewarned, nevertheless by around 0900 hrs on 1 January Allied aircraft were already aloft going about their 'normal' business, mounting patrols or performing actual fighter-bomber missions against German tactical targets. This meant that the *Jagdflieger* were heading towards an enemy that was already alert. Any thoughts that most, if not all, Allied pilots would be on the ground recovering from New Year's Eve festivities were incorrect.

The first of many Bf 109s to fall that day had been lost even before the opening *Bodenplatte* attacks had taken place. It is now generally accepted that one of the first, if not the first, contact with the incoming Luftwaffe units was made by two Spitfires from No 2 Sqn. This famous unit was one of the RAF's premier fighter-reconnaissance squadrons, and it was equipped with Griffon-engined Spitfire XIVs. Flying from the Dutch airfield of Gilze-Rijen (B77), Flt Lts L J Packwood and J M Young

The aftermath of the attack by JG 27 and IV./JG 54 on Brussels-Melsbroek on 1 January – the remains of a B-25 smoulders as a fire crew struggles to dampen the flames. The fighters from both units destroyed more than 50 aircraft here, although 17 Bf 109s and three Fw 190s were in turn shot down and 13 pilots killed and three captured (*Tony Holmes Collection*)

were reconnoitring the Leeuwen–Hilversum–Arnhem area when they sighted a large Luftwaffe formation at 0905 hrs. It was heading for Brussels-Melsbroek (B58) airfield, and consisted of two pathfinder Ju 88s and a mixed force of Bf 109s and Fw 190s, including the Messerschmitts of JG 27's I. and II. *Gruppen* that had taken off from Rheine at 0825 hrs.

The RAF pilots assumed that the fighters were escorting the twin-engined Junkers, and although heavily outnumbered, they immediately attacked. One of the Bf 109s was being flown by Unteroffizier Heinrich Braun of 2./JG 27. In the ensuing engagement he was shot down and killed, his Messerschmitt crashing east of Utrecht. Packwood, who was flying Spitfire XIV RM708, subsequently wrote in his combat report;

'We turned up-sun of the formation and attacked the last section. I attacked an Me 109 from dead astern and above, the enemy aircraft taking no evasive action. I gave it a five-second burst with cannon and machine guns, closing from 400 to 150 yards. I observed strikes on the cockpit and fuselage, and the enemy aircraft disintegrated. The starboard wing broke off and the aircraft flicked over onto its back and hit the ground in flames.'

Although Braun's demise was viewed by other pilots in the formation, they could do nothing. The whole purpose was to reach the intended target, not to become embroiled in aerial combat on the way. Writing after the *Bodenplatte* events, Oberleutnant Emil Clade of Hesepe-based III./JG 27, which was also part of the attacking force, explained 'We had orders not to interfere in a dogfight'. Indeed, the instructions given to many (but seemingly not all) pilots included the necessity to maintain strict radio silence until they were returning to base and over friendly territory.

Despite the loss of Unteroffizier Braun, JG 27 subsequently made one of the most noteworthy attacks of the whole *Bodenplatte* operation. Along with the Fw 190s of IV./JG 54, the *Geschwader*'s aircraft successfully strafed the airfield in repeated attacks. Brussels-Melsbroek (B58) was a major RAF base and home to several frontline squadrons, in addition to being an important destination for personnel visiting the Belgian capital and Allied headquarters. Three 2nd TAF Mitchell units, Nos 98, 180 and 320 Sqns, all had aircraft destroyed, as did Mosquito-equipped No 140 Sqn. At least five Spitfire PR XIs from No 16 Sqn were lost, while No 69 Sqn's Wellingtons were badly hit, with at least 11 destroyed. Several visiting aircraft were similarly written off, and many surviving machines (operational and visiting) were damaged.

This was a spectacular success for the attackers, but the price was high – JG 27 lost 17 aircraft in total, including 11 pilots killed and three captured. Similarly, IV./JG 54 lost three, with two pilots killed. Four of the attacking fighters were claimed by the airfield's anti-aircraft defences.

However, these successes was not mirrored elsewhere. The attack by Bf 109-equipped JG 77 on Antwerp-Duerne (B70) followed several disastrous days in December 1944 during which the *Geschwader* suffered many losses and had seen two of its airfields (Essen-Mühlheim and Düsseldorf-Lohausen) badly damaged during specifically targeted air raids. Ironically Antwerp-Duerne was one of the most populous Allied airfields in terms of units stationed there. Principal users were five Typhoon fighter-bomber squadrons of the RAF's No 146 Wing, which should have been a prize target for the Germans.

Based at Dortmund, I. and II./JG 77 took off at approximately 0800 hrs, and were joined by III./JG 77, whose Messerschmitts had departed from Bönninghardt-Süd at roughly the same time. The formation was led by two pathfinder Ju 88G nightfighters. Fired on by German flak prior to even reaching the frontline, the JG 77 formation became lost. It appears that some aircraft made an impromptu attack on Woensdrecht (B79) Advanced Landing Ground (ALG) instead of Antwerp-Duerne. Some JG 77 pilots located their assigned target by themselves, attacking parked aircraft on the airfield and destroying six Typhoons. The airfield was also apparently strafed in a random attack by some Bf 109s from JG 26 that were seemingly lost.

Several JG 77 pilots, unable to find the airfield, attacked 'targets of opportunity' in the environs of Antwerp instead. This was a bad idea, for the area was thick with anti-aircraft defences tasked with protecting the city against V1 'flying bomb' attacks. Amongst those killed was Leutnant Heinrich Hackler, the *Staffelkapitän* of 11./JG 77 who was leading III. *Gruppe* that day. A veteran member of JG 77 who had flown with the unit since 1940, he had been credited with 56 aerial victories and was awarded the Knight's Cross of the Iron Cross in August 1944.

Hackler was one of a number of experienced pilots from several units who were either killed or taken prisoner during *Bodenplatte* – losses which were a significant blow to the Luftwaffe. For the destruction of around 12 Allied aircraft at Duerne, JG 77 had 11 Messerschmitts shot down or lost to accidents, with six pilots killed. At least one of the *Geschwader*'s pathfinder Ju 88G nightfighters was also shot down.

The newest Bf 109 unit that participated in *Bodenplatte* was JG 6, which had formed during the latter half of 1944 with personnel drawn mainly from Bf 110/Me 410-equipped ZG 26. With the Bf 110 now basically obsolete as a day air-to-ground platform, the *Stab* of the new JG 6 (with Oberstleutnant Johann Kogler as *Geschwaderkommodore*) was formed at Königsberg-Devau theoretically with a mix of Bf 109Gs and Fw 190As. In effect, JG 6 was principally an Fw 190 operator, but its third *Gruppe* flew Bf 109Gs. The latter had been formed during October 1944 at Schwerin-Görries from I./JG 5, with the experienced Hauptmann Theo Weissenberger at the helm.

The intended target for JG 6 during *Bodenplatte* was the highly important Allied airfield of Volkel (B80) in the Netherlands. This was a major air base, and it was comparatively close to the frontline. The base was home to many fighter-bombers including Typhoons and Tempest Vs. It was, therefore, one of the prime targets for the Luftwaffe. The fact that such a major airfield was entrusted to a comparatively new unit with a number of inexperienced pilots that had already suffered maulings from Allied fighters while on Reich defence duty is somewhat perplexing.

The unit's various *Staffeln* were scattered over a number of airfields in the Quackenbrück area of Germany, and for *Bodenplatte* JG 6 reported no fewer than 99 aircraft available for the attack on Volkel. As with other *Geschwader*, the majority of pilots listed to take part were briefed the day before, although most of the unit commanders were aware of the intended target prior to this.

Unfortunately for JG 6, many things went wrong. To begin with, an Fw 190 from I. *Gruppe* crashed on take-off at Delmenhorst, killing its pilot. Proceeding westwards at an altitude of just 70 m, the large JG 6 formation apparently made the correct turns as indicated by the Ju 88G Lotse that was leading them. Their planned course, however, took them over the recently constructed airfield of Heesch (B88), which the Germans were seemingly unaware of. This was a fatal mistake, for resident at B88 was the Royal Canadian Air Force's No 126 Wing, with its five Spitfire squadrons.

Several Spitfires were already airborne to fulfil their 'normal' armed reconnaissance sorties of the day, and others were preparing to take-off, when the huge formation of Bf 109s and Fw 190s swept over the airfield, apparently completely oblivious to its existence. The pilot of one of the last aircraft in the formation must have realised that they were over-flying an Allied airfield for he hastily opened fire, but inflicted no significant damage. Heesch's anti-aircraft defences reacted to greater effect, shooting down a Bf 109 from JG 3 that was supposed to be attacking Eindhoven (B78) airfield.

Although it was a hurried, ragged take-off, ten Spitfires of No 401 Sqn immediately became airborne and gave chase to the JG 6 formation. In a matter of minutes Flg Off Doug Cameron had shot down at least two, possibly three, of the Messerschmitts. One of his victims was Unteroffizier Karl Betz of 10./JG 6 in Bf 109G-10 'Black 10', who was killed when his aircraft dived into the ground and exploded.

Further Spitfires intercepted the JG 6 formation, including some that had been heading home to Heesch at the end of their armed patrols. The confusion that resulted from the Canadian Spitfire attacks appears to have caused Oberstleutnant Kogler to lead the formation too far south, causing them to miss a vital turn. Lost, JG 6 broke up when some of the

Fw 190A pilots from I. *Gruppe* witnessed the smoke from JG 3's attack on Eindhoven and departed to join in, presumably thinking that this was Volkel. The Messerschmitts of III./JG 6 were thrown into disarray when accurate anti-aircraft fire destroyed the Bf 109G of their leader, Major Helmut Kühle, who was killed when his fighter crashed northwest of Helmond.

Another part of the JG 6 formation located the airfield at Helmond (B86), which was under construction and had no resident flying units. In the subsequent completely pointless attack, accurate anti-aircraft fire from the resident RAF Regiment gunners shot down Oberstleutnant Kogler. Wounded, he crash-landed his Fw 190A-9 and was taken prisoner.

Soon Allied fighters were arriving from different directions to intercept the scattered JG 6 fighters. Tempest V pilot Flg Off D J Butcher of Volkel-based No 3 Sqn caught up with a fleeing Bf 109 and together with his wingman shot it down. The Messerschmitt was probably that of Unteroffizier Hans Schaupp of 10./JG 6, who was killed when his Bf 109G-14/AS crashed near Helmond. A number of other dogfights ensued between Spitfires and Tempest Vs and the Bf 109s and Fw 190s of JG 6.

While these took place, Volkel airfield itself suffered only minor attacks from lost German aircraft, allowing this valuable location to operate normally. JG 6 had completely failed to put the base out of action, and had paid a very high price. Although the figures are open to reinterpretation, and some pilots remain unaccounted for even to this day, the unit seemingly lost 28 fighters, with 16 pilots killed or missing. The Messerschmitts of III./JG 6 came off worst, losing 12 of the 20 assigned, including the fighter flown by its *Gruppenkommandeur*, Major Kühle.

With JG 6's *Geschwaderkommodore*, Oberstleutnant Kogler, a PoW, leadership of the *Geschwader* passed to the experienced Major Gerhard Barkhorn. Soon after, JG 6 was removed from frontline operations in the West and sent instead to the Eastern Front.

Amongst the most experienced Bf 109 units that were involved in *Bodenplatte* was the veteran JG 26. Already familiar with Bf 109E/F *Jabo* operations in the West from earlier in the war, this *Geschwader* had since become yet another to be embroiled in Reich defence duties against USAAF heavy bombers. By late 1944, however, only III./JG 26 was still flying Messerschmitts, the other component *Gruppen* of the unit having long since converted to the Fw 190. For *Bodenplatte*, JG 26 was assigned two separate airfields, with part of the *Geschwader* targeting Grimbergen (B66) along with Fw 190-equipped III./JG 54. On 1 January, however, Grimbergen was devoid of flying units. Several squadrons from Polish-manned No 131 Wing were due to move in, but they had yet to arrive.

The Messerschmitts of III./JG 26, which were based at Plantlünne, were tasked with attacking Brussels-Evere (B56). This airfield was known to several of the unit's airmen because elements of JG 26 had been temporarily based there several months earlier while retreating from the advancing Allies. Curiously, bearing in mind the lack of awareness of most pilots involved in *Bodenplatte* until the last minute, some of III./JG 26's pilots were briefed several days beforehand as to their intended target. A sand model was made of Evere airfield, although the location's name was not specified. Nevertheless, the pilots recognised it without difficulty.

Resident at Evere were the Spitfires of No 127 Wing, this Canadian-manned unit being led by none other than Wg Cdr Johnnie Johnson. But not all of the Canadian squadrons making up his command were in residence at Evere on 1 January, with some being at RAF Warmwell for an armament practice camp. The airfield was also home to an eclectic collection of communications aircraft. Also temporarily resident were various US heavy bombers that had landed there after sustaining damage or experiencing technical problems while on operations. The latter were of far less military value than the priceless fighters of No 127 Wing, and were typical of 'walking wounded' bombers that were found at many Allied airfields in the vicinity.

The attack on Brussels-Evere was carried out by Fw 190D-9-equipped II./JG 26 based at Klausheide and III./JG 26 from Plantlünne with its mix of Bf 109G-14 and K-4 fighters. Led by Hauptmann Walter Krupinski, the latter unit's Messerschmitts took off at around 0820 hrs behind two Ju 88G nightfighter Lotsen. Unfortunately for the Germans, a lot went wrong. Confusion exists to this day as to the exact circumstances, but it appears that after take-off Hauptmann Krupinski with his *Stabsschwarm* and one of the Ju 88Gs became detached from the rest of the *Gruppe*, and he eventually returned to Plantlünne without having reached Evere. It has been claimed that his Messerschmitt had been hit and slightly damaged by anti-aircraft fire.

The rest of III./JG 26 formed up on the second Ju 88G and headed for their target. Like other units, the pilots flew very low and took a circuitous route so as not to signal their intentions, and to avoid the flak around built-up areas or military installations. Nonetheless, four Messerschmitts were shot down en route, at least one by German anti-aircraft defences before they had crossed into Allied airspace.

Led for much of the way to their target by the Ju 88G Lotse, the Messerschmitts of III./JG 26 arrived at Evere at roughly the same time as the Fw 190D-9s of II./JG 26. The attack began at 0926 hrs. Already airborne were two Spitfires of No 403 Sqn undertaking an armed weather reconnaissance over the frontline. Two more Spitfires from that unit had also just taken off, while No 416 Sqn was at readiness, awaiting the word to scramble.

The two Spitfire pilots just departing Evere spotted the incoming Luftwaffe raiders, and one of them immediately turned to engage the fighters. Their two squadronmates, by then already some way away, also altered course to join the fray as soon as it was clear that the massed arrival of fighters was hostile and not friendly. Several rapid dogfights ensued in which three Messerschmitts were claimed shot down.

Less fortunate were the No 416 Sqn Spitfires. Leading the unit's take-off was Flt Lt Dave Harling, who had just become airborne when the Germans arrived over the airfield. In the ensuing melee, he destroyed an Fw 190 moments before he too was shot down and killed. His squadronmates quickly vacated their Spitfires on the taxiways and found whatever cover they could in fox-holes and trenches while the attack on the airfield commenced.

In the following 30 minutes or so, the JG 26 pilots very effectively shot up Evere, with many of them making several strafing runs. The airfield's defences were not as efficient as at other bases and the German pilots were very successful in destroying many aircraft and much ground equipment. One *Jagdflieger* was seen by watching Allied servicemen to make several strafing runs without being fired on. He even succeeded in destroying a parked aircraft inside a hangar during one of his passes.

The successful attack by II. and III./JG 26 resulted in Evere only returning to something like 'normal' after nine days, although operations began to be flown on 3 January. Some 61 Allied aircraft were destroyed there, plus vehicles and infrastructure. These losses in aircraft and equipment were easily made good, however, as there were ample supplies reaching the Continent from England by then. As was seen at other *Bodenplatte* targets, some of the German pilots had concentrated on the larger aircraft present, including transports and the worthless crippled and scrapped four-engined bombers acting as decoys, instead of the far more important fighters. One of the victims was the personal Dakota transport of Air Marshal Sir Arthur Coningham, commander of 2nd TAF, together with other communications types which were of little value to the overall picture of the war.

Most affected was No 416 Sqn, which lost the majority of its Spitfires on the flightline. The unit's diarist summed up the destruction somewhat laconically;

'The year started with a bang, and what a bang. The Jerries had the finger well out and pulled a surprise raid on us.'

The journey home was less than straightforward for the German pilots. At least two Messerschmitts were lost, including the aircraft of Leutnant Gottfried Meier of 9./JG 26, who died when his 'White 15' crashed near the Belgian village of Vrasene after apparently being shot down by anti-aircraft fire. Total losses recorded by III./JG 26 were six Messerschmitts during the raid. The success of the attack on Evere by II./JG 26 with its Fw 190s and the Bf 109-equipped III./JG 26 was in stark contrast to the raid against the almost empty Grimbergen by the Fw 190s of I./JG 26 and IV./JG 54, which suffered considerable losses for the little that was gained there.

CONFUSED ATTACKS

Resident at the Belgian airfield of St Trond (A92) were the P-47D-equipped 48th and 404th FGs of the Ninth Air Force. This airfield was near to the frontlines, and it boasted comparatively primitive conditions and a large number of light anti-aircraft batteries to defend the base. Detailed to attack this important target were the Fw 190s of SG 4 and the Bf 109s and Fw 190s of JG 2. One of the most famous of all the Luftwaffe fighter units, JG 2 had also been involved in *Jabo* missions against England, as detailed earlier in this book. By late 1944, only its II. *Gruppe* at Nidda was still operational with Bf 109s, its other *Gruppen* and *Stab* being equipped with Fw 190s. For *Bodenplatte*, II. *Gruppe* could field both Bf 109G-14s and a few of the rarer Bf 109K-4s. The *Gruppenkommandeur* was Hauptmann Georg Schröder.

In the event, the attack against St Trond on 1 January was a completely confused affair in which SG 4 and JG 2 were joined by elements of JG 4 that were supposed to be striking at Le Culot (A89) but became completely lost. There were so many Allied airfields in roughly the same area that even if one was missed, another would not be far away.

Take-off for II./JG 2's Messerschmitts at Nidda was at approximately 0825 hrs. This *Gruppe* was able to sortie 20 fighters, 13 of which were Bf 109G-14s. After forming up, they joined the Fw 190s of other elements of JG 2 on their designated course, crossing the frontline near to Malmedy. At that point the JG 2 formation was subjected to a substantial barrage of anti-aircraft fire from US Army units. They had flown over a very active part of the frontline where much bitter fighting had already taken place. It was also near an area known as 'Buzz Bomb Alley' due to the V1s that were being aimed at the port of Antwerp. The anti-aircraft units were numerous and already active, resulting in a number of JG 2's fighters being shot down.

Although the Focke-Wulfs were particularly hard hit, the II. *Gruppe* Messerschmitts were a little more fortunate. Nonetheless, the *Gruppenkommandeur*, Hauptmann Georg Schröder, was shot down and captured – at least three other Bf 109 pilots were also lost. By then the JG 2 formation was in disarray and totally scattered. Some pilots attacked ground targets of opportunity and then headed back to Germany, while others pressed on singly or in pairs towards St Trond. Eventually, several made strafing runs against parked aircraft. However, it appears that, completely lost, they actually targeted Asch (Y29) and Ophoven (Y32) airfields instead, joining in with the attacks against those airfields which were the responsibility of other units.

II./JG 2's tally of five fighters lost and three damaged was light compared to the Fw 190s of other *Gruppen* of JG 2, who suffered very high casualties. Altogether JG 2 lost 43 aircraft, with 12 damaged. Added to this was the almost total failure of SG 4 to form up, this unit eventually aborting their mission altogether. Thus, the attack on St Trond by JG 2 and SG 4 was a total failure. However, St Trond *was* attacked, but by pilots who should have been elsewhere. They were from JG 4.

Another of the more recently formed *Geschwader*, JG 4 had only come into being during June–July 1944 under the command of the experienced Major Gerhard Michalski. The unit's Messerschmitt-equipped *Gruppen* were I., III. and IV., whilst its II. *Gruppe* was a *Sturm* outfit flying anti-bomber Fw 190s. The Messerschmitts were mostly based at Darmstadt-Griesheim, but IV. *Gruppe* flew from Frankfurt/Rhein-Main.

The designated targets for JG 4 were the two airfields of Le Culot, the principal airfield being A89, later better-known as Beauvechain, and the smaller Le Culot East (Y10). These bases were home to the 36th and 373rd FGs, both flying Thunderbolts, and the camera-equipped elements (mainly F-5 Lightnings) of the 363rd Tactical Reconnaissance Group. All three groups were assigned to the Ninth Air Force. Both airfields were therefore very important locations in the overall *Bodenplatte* strategy.

Like many other units, JG 4's take-off was at approximately 0820 hrs, although the *Sturm* Fw 190s left a little earlier. Similar to JG 2, the *Geschwader*'s formation flew over the frontline near Malmedy and was subjected to intense Allied anti-aircraft fire. This successfully broke up the individual formations, with one of the Lotse Ju 88Gs being destroyed in addition to several Messerschmitts and Focke-Wulfs. One of the pilots shot down was Feldwebel Karl Berg of 15./JG 4 in his Bf 109K-4 'Yellow 4' – similar to a number of Luftwaffe pilots who were lost during *Bodenplatte*, no trace was ever found of him and he has no known grave.

In the confusion the entire III. *Gruppe* formation returned to base. Its commander, Hauptmann Friedrich Eberle, appears to have subsequently been court-martialled due to his unit's failure to attack its assigned target.

In total, JG 4 lost 26 aircraft, with six others damaged, and its aircraft never found their allotted target. Interestingly, in his monthly summary of operations, *Geschwaderkommodore* Major Gerhard Michalski described *Bodenplatte* as follows;

'Special Operation – With the goal of destroying the Allied fighter and bomber units stationed in the Dutch–Belgian area, the units of 3. and 8. *Jagddivision* flew a special operation on January 1, 1945. This operation had been in preparation since the beginning of December. *Jagdgeschwader* 4 had the assignment to attack the airfield of Le Culot, southeast of Brussels, with all *Gruppen*. To make orientation easier and to make sure that the target was reached, each *Gruppe*

Major Gerhard Michalski's JG 4 lost 26 aircraft on 1 January, with the bulk of them being Bf 109s. The *Jagdgeschwader*'s performance in *Bodenplatte* was quite dismal, as the unit failed to attack either of its allocated targets (*Tony Holmes Collection*)

would be led by one or two Ju 88 Lotse. This meant that the pilots would not need to navigate, and could concentrate on their position in the formation and low-level flying. *Kommodore* JG 4 would lead IV./JG 4. All other *Gruppen* would be led by their *Kommandeure* or their second in commands'.

He made no mention of the subsequent complete failure of the mission, which meant the two Le Culot airfields were never attacked. However, some of the Thunderbolts stationed there did encounter Luftwaffe fighters while performing their pre-briefed fighter-bomber mission of the day.

At around 1000 hrs over Limburg, 1Lt Paul J Walsh of the 373rd FG's 412th FS spotted an enemy aircraft. He and other members of his squadron were flying Thunderbolts armed with a single 500-lb bomb and fragmentation cluster bombs under each wing. Walsh explained what happened next in his combat report;

'I was flying "Turmoil Blue Three" without a wingman on Mission V89-3. "Roselee" [the ground-based fighter controller] vectored us all over the sky to intercept enemy aircraft. "Red Number 3" called in one "bogey" at "six o'clock low". I identified the enemy aircraft as a Me 109 and made a bounce from 8000 to 3500 ft out of the sun, having jettisoned my bombs as soon as I was positive of the contact's identity and I was about ready to fire.

'My first pass was from about 15 degrees down to about five degrees. I observed many hits as the enemy aircraft took evasive action in the clouds. I waited on top for him to pop out again, and I got three good bursts in. I observed hits, but these were dead astern shots and I couldn't get him to [catch

Although a relatively substantial amount of damage was caused at St Trond by JG 4's impromptu attack, it did not stop the resident Thunderbolt-equipped 48th and 404th FGs from continuing with their operations on 1 January. This burning P-47D was probably one of the casualties from amongst the 48th FG's Thunderbolts that were caught on the ground (*Malcolm V Lowe Collection*)

on] fire. He ducked in the clouds again and I waited below the strata (the lowest part was at about 100 ft). He popped out and I got a few hits and observed another Me 109 flying to the right of him. I called "Turmoil Leader", repeating my vector (150) and number of aircraft.

'At this time I saw three P-47s being mistaken for Fw 190s. The enemy aircraft, including presumably his wingman, turned into the other planes. I got a good burst in and saw hits as his canopy flew off. I didn't shoot at the other Me 109, figuring he was leading me into a bounce. It was impossible for me to investigate the crash, but I do believe the pilot bailed out. There was some black smoke coming from the plane prior to the time I saw the jettisoned canopy. He disappeared in the clouds and I pulled away from the other aircraft, climbed through the overcast and saw that the planes were P-47s trying to locate a target for the rest of the squadron orbiting over the overcast. I claim one Me 109 destroyed.'

1Lt Walsh's claim was not allowed. Other members of the squadron did, however, accomplish their intended fighter-bomber mission by attacking a railway marshalling yard near Euskirchen. The German fighters had not distracted the squadron from its original purpose, and no aircraft were lost from 1Lt Walsh's formation.

Although the intended raid on the two Le Culot airfields never took place, nonetheless, several JG 4 pilots pressed on, determined to fulfil their mission. Completely lost, they stumbled upon and attacked St Trond instead. This impromptu JG 4 attack force amounted to seven or eight aircraft, although some published sources have claimed that 12 fighters were involved. They were led over their new target by Oberleutnant Lothar Wolff, who had taken temporary leadership of the IV./JG 4 formation when Major Michalski had returned to base apparently with engine trouble. Wolff was convinced that they had arrived at Le Culot, but they were actually at St Trond! During the subsequent attack, the Messerschmitts were joined by at least two Fw 190s from II./JG 4, who were equally lost.

At St Trond, the 492nd and 493rd FSs of the 48th FG were making ready for their first missions of the day. The Messerschmitts arrived at approximately 0915 hrs and proceeded to shoot up the 48th FG's dispersal area. Pilots rapidly exited their aircraft and joined their groundcrews in any foxholes or trenches that were available. The Germans subsequently caused a considerable amount of destruction in that part of the airfield. However, several damaged and militarily worthless B-17s and at least one B-24 were also attacked. Located in the centre of the airfield, these 'heavies' acted as very successful decoys and had no real value as they were already virtually wrecks.

The local defences, which were mainly light anti-aircraft batteries armed with 0.50-in. machine guns, swung into action. An Fw 190 apparently still carrying its underfuselage drop tank was rapidly shot down, its pilot pulling up his flaming aircraft and taking to his parachute. A Bf 109 was hit directly over the airfield and it crashed beside the main runway, killing 20-year-old Oberfähnrich Horst Grüner of 15./JG 4. Bf 109G-14/AS Wk-Nr 461200 'Yellow 13' flown by Oberfähnrich Arnolf Russow, who was the wingman of Oberleutnant Wolff, was also hit by anti-aircraft fire and belly landed not far from St Trond airfield. Curiously, after the pilot had been captured, his aircraft was then buried by local inhabitants.

USAAF personnel survey a burnt-out wreck at St Trond in the aftermath of the *Bodenplatte* attack by JG 4's Messerschmitts and Focke-Wulfs, which should have been raiding Le Culot airfield instead. The destroyed aircraft is believed to be Bf 109K-4 Wk-Nr 331473 of Oberfahnrich Horst Grüner of 15./JG 4, which was shot down by the airfield's defences and crashed beside the runway, killing the pilot (*Malcolm V Lowe Collection*)

Only two of the JG 4 fighters (both from IV. *Gruppe*) that attacked St Trond regained German-held territory. One of them was flown by Oberleutnant Wolff, who was the only pilot to actually fly all the way back to Rhein-Main.

The handful of JG 4 fighters that had targeted St Trond left considerable damage in their wake. The 492nd FS had three Thunderbolts destroyed and ten damaged, while the 494th FS lost two fighters and had four more damaged. The 404th FG, located in a different part of the airfield, was less heavily hit, with its 506th FS having only one P-47 destroyed and four damaged and the 506th and 507th FSs suffering damage to five Thunderbolts between them. There was also some limited destruction of infrastructure. Despite these losses, the two resident fighter groups mounted their intended missions later that day.

Many airmen and groundcrew had tales to tell of the encounter. Capt Floyd Blair of the 507th FS was making his way to the briefing for his next sortie when the JG 4 attack started;

'I was scheduled for the mission that had a take-off time of 1144 hrs. As you will see, we made the mission. I was down on the flightline heading for the briefing when I heard all the racket and was looking around and people were running for cover. I looked in the direction of the noise. It was while I was looking for the source of the racket that I saw the ugly nose of an ME 109 heading straight at me. Just as he started firing I was heading with great haste for the dugout that was practically in front of me, and I took advantage of this and leapt into it just as he was passing over. Obviously, he missed me. I went on to the briefing for my mission, and flew it as scheduled.'

Writing the 404th FG's diary entry for January 1945, Maj Robert W Manss, the group's Historical Officer, had this to say about JG 4's attack on St Trond;

'New Year's Greetings were extended to the 404th by the Luftwaffe in the form of a strafing by six to eight planes on the morning of 1 January. The first warning came to all personnel by the rat tat tat and booming of the field's ack ack defense. However, very few actually saw the Jerry planes, except perhaps the Anti-Aircraft defense, for everyone jumped into the nearest hole and took cover until five of the planes had been shot down and the last one had left the vicinity. The Group was very fortunate in not having any personnel injured, and all damage to the aircraft was quickly repaired and they were operational again. A good story of the attack on Site A-92 is given in the Annex to the XXIX TAC A-2 Periodic Report No. 90, dated 2 January 1945, which follows:

'"Between 0920 and 0945 hrs on 1 January 1945, Site A-92 underwent strafing attacks by seven FW 190s and ME 109s. The attacking squadron made three or four attacks across the field, inflicting damage to combat and administrative aircraft. Ten aircraft were destroyed and 31 damaged. No air personnel were killed or seriously wounded, though it is believed one anti-aircraft soldier was killed and several were wounded. The enemy aircraft were engaged by anti-aircraft fire, and the destruction of four has been confirmed, one other is claimed destroyed and one damaged.

'"The attack was well planned and came with no warning of the approach of hostiles. Information obtained from documents in crashed aircraft indicates the original target was Site A-89. The approach was across the battle line at St Vith thence to Huy and then the airfield. Either the plans were changed or the aircraft were off course as no attack was made on A89 [Le Culot] during the day. One reason for the lack of advance warning was the fact that the enemy aircraft came all the way on the deck and no plots were obtained. The first visual observations were not made sufficiently early to enable a warning to be given.

'"It is believed from the tactics employed that the squadron was led by an experienced pilot and that the remainder were young and inexperienced. The leader got away, and his flying was reported as being far superior to the others. After completing a strafing run, he would make a tight low-level turn, while the others did not turn as tightly or at as low an altitude. All anti-aircraft claims were made on hits inflicted during the turns. Some of the enemy aircraft were carrying belly tanks, but no bombs were dropped or observed. At no time during the attack did the altitude exceed 500 ft.

'"Pilots taken as prisoners appear unusually security conscious, and apparently the attack was extremely well conceived and carried out. Excellent R/T [radio] discipline added materially to the element of surprise."

'Undoubtedly the New Year's Greetings extended to the 404th on 1 January 1945 will remain in the memories of all personnel for many years to come on New Year's Day in the future.'

Only two French airfields were specified for attack during *Bodenplatte*. These were Étain (A82, also sometimes called Verdun) and Metz-Frescaty (Y34), both in northeastern France near the border with Belgium. They were assigned as *Bodenplatte* targets to Bf 109-operating JG 53, although they were at extreme range for the unit's Messerschmitts, which were based in and around the Stuttgart region of Germany. JG 53 was one of the most active Bf 109 units, operating the type throughout World War 2. By late 1944 the *Geschwader* had a mix of Bf 109G-14s and G-14/ASs, together with some Bf 109K-4s. Its *Stab* was located at Stuttgart-Echterdingen, I. *Gruppe* at Veszprem, in Hungary (and therefore not involved in *Bodenplatte*), II. *Gruppe* at Malmsheim, III. *Gruppe* at Kirrlach and IV. *Gruppe* at Stuttgart-Echterdingen (with 13. *Staffel* at Nellingen).

The tactical US Ninth Air Force had a very strong presence in northeastern France during the closing weeks of 1944. Supporting the US Third Army in the Metz-Saar area was XIX TAC with its fighter-bombers, mainly P-47Ds. Based at Étain was the Thunderbolt-equipped 362nd FG, while at Metz-Frescaty was the 365th FG, which had been brought in from Chièvres (A84), in Belgium, to bolster the aerial effort against the German ground offensive. This meant there were major targets at both airfields for the incoming JG 53 Messerschmitts.

Like all participants in *Bodenplatte*, the *Geschwader*'s Bf 109s carried a 300-litre drop tank beneath the fuselage to give them sufficient range to reach their target airfields and back, but in the case of JG 53 this was particularly necessary. Radio silence was strictly enforced, which proved to be a complete disaster for III. *Gruppe*. Taking off at 0830 hrs from Kirrlach and following their Lotse Ju 88G nightfighter, the low-flying formation was still over German-held territory when it was bounced by Thunderbolts from the 358th FG's 367th FS.

The squadron's 12 P-47Ds, led by Capt Winton Perry, had taken off from Toul-Croix de Metz (A90) at 0810 hrs on an armed reconnaissance mission, the Thunderbolts carrying a single 500-lb bomb beneath each wing. They headed for the Zweibrücken–Homburg area, where some dropped their bombs on various targets while watched over by their fellow pilots from above. En route, they encountered the III./JG 53 formation heading for Étain. With the advantage of surprise and height, the latter allowing the USAAF pilots to dive at the Germans from 'out of the sun', the 367th easily prevailed in the one-sided encounter that ensued.

In a matter of minutes the III. *Gruppe* formation had been completely scattered, individual pilots doing the best they could to escape their American opponents. Having jettisoned their drop tanks, there was no way that they could attack Étain and return to base. The Americans claimed 13 shot down, one probable and six damaged. 1Lt Wayne Owers claimed three and Capt Perry two.

The fleeing German fighters were then spotted by pilots of the 358th FG's 366th FS, also from Toul-Croix de Metz, who had taken off shortly after the 367th FS and were on their own armed reconnaissance mission. They shot down a further Messerschmitt. In a final encounter, the 365th FS (the third squadron of the 358th FG), which had taken off just prior to the 367th FS, encountered the two Lotsen Ju 88Gs

For small gain, many Messerschmitts were shot down during *Bodenplatte*, further reducing the depleted ranks of the *Jagdwaffe* fighter force. Unteroffizier Herbert Maxis of 13./JG 53 force landed his Bf 109G-14/AS Wk-Nr 784993 'White 13' after duelling with an anti-aircraft battery. As he climbed out of the aircraft he raised his hands to surrender, but was immediately shot dead by a member of 'A' Battery of the 739th Field Artillery Battalion. His aircraft proved to be a curiosity, and was much photographed in the following days (*Malcolm V Lowe Collection*)

that had intended to guide III./JG 53 to Étain. 1Lt Donald Flowers shot one down and damaged the other.

Étain was thus spared from attack. Metz-Frescaty, however, was not so lucky. The *Stab* and IV./JG 53 at Stuttgart-Echterdingen, plus 13./JG 53 at Nellingen, took off just after 0800 hrs, with II./JG 53 following at around 0835 hrs from Malmsheim. The force consisted of around 48 Messerschmitts, including a small number of Bf 109K-4s.

On the way, the two separate formations were engaged by several US Army anti-aircraft batteries, which downed at least four Messerschmitts. Some of the German pilots broke formation and fought with the batteries, leading to unnecessary losses.

Amongst those shot down was Unteroffizier Herbert Maxis of 13./JG 53, who belly landed his 'White 13' after duelling with an anti-aircraft installation. As he climbed out of the aircraft he raised his hands to surrender, but was immediately shot dead by a member of 'A' Battery of the 739th Field Artillery Battalion. Also lost was Fahnrich Siegfried Leese of 14./JG 53. At 19 years of age, he was one of the youngest pilots engaged in the *Bodenplatte* operation.

Nevertheless, having jettisoned their drop tanks, *Stab* and IV./JG 53 arrived over Metz at approximately 0915 hrs, where they were targeted by accurate anti-aircraft fire. The defences at the airfield were ready and waiting for them. Leading by example the *Geschwaderkommodore*, Oberstleutnant Helmut Bennemann, commenced the shooting up of the 365th FG's 386th FS Thunderbolts as they sat in the unit's dispersal area being prepared for their first sorties of the day. However, his Messerschmitt immediately took hits, although Bennemann was able to fly away. Two of the following Bf 109s were not so fortunate, being shot down over the airfield. One of the pilots involved, Oberfeldwebel Stefan Kohl of 13./JG 53, hastily exited his Bf 109G-14 'White 11' in what was his fourth, and definitely last, bail out. He was captured soon after landing.

Arriving at roughly the same time were the Messerschmitts of II./JG 53, which joined in the strafing of the airfield. Although the anti-aircraft defences were highly efficient, the Bf 109s still managed to inflict considerable destruction on the aircraft at Metz. At least 22 Thunderbolts were destroyed and many others damaged. Worst hit was the 386th FS, but aircraft from all three squadrons were destroyed. Fortunately, the 365th FG's 387th and 388th FSs had already taken off and were away from the airfield. They returned too late to catch the now-fleeing Messerschmitts, which headed for home as soon as possible, bearing in mind their precarious fuel state.

On the return journey the *Geschwader* lost further aircraft. Several were shot down by Allied anti-aircraft batteries, while others simply ran out of fuel and had to crash-land. Some pilots regained German-held territory but had to land at other airfields. Oberstleutnant Helmut Bennemann successfully reached Stuttgart-Echterdingen, but his JG 53 had been badly hit. Altogether, 30 Messerschmitts were lost from the attack force of approximately 80 fighters. Although the aircraft losses were made up comparatively quickly, the 13 pilots killed or missing, with others captured, hit JG 53 hard. For the Ninth Air Force, the destruction of 22 P-47s was a temporary blow. Indeed, within seven days the 365th FG had returned to full strength. There was no shortage of Thunderbolts, or pilots to fly them, at that late stage in the war.

A Oberstleutnant Helmut Bennemann, the final *Geschwaderkommodore* of JG 53, led the highly effective attack on Metz-Frescaty that saw at least 22 Thunderbolts destroyed. His Bf 109 was hit by anti-aircraft fire whilst strafing the airfield, but he still managed to make it back to Stuttgart-Echterdingen (*Tony Holmes Collection*)

The attack by JG 11 against Asch (Y29), situated near Genk in Belgium, was another major operation. Conditions were primitive at this Allied outpost, which was a recently constructed ALG that boasted meagre facilities. Resident with the Thunderbolt-equipped 366th FG of the Ninth Air Force, together was a contingent of P-51Ds from the Eighth Air Force's 352nd FG. The Mustangs had been sent on detachment to the Continent from their usual base at RAF Raydon, in Essex, on 23 December to help bolster the Allied aerial effort in that area. Tragically, it had already proved to be a costly deployment, for on Christmas Day US Army anti-aircraft batteries had shot down two Mustangs in error. Although one of the pilots survived, the other did not – he was none other than Maj George Preddy, the USAAF's top-scoring Mustang pilot. His death was a terrible blow to the 352nd.

Equipped with both Fw 190s and Bf 109s, JG 11 had already flown in support of German ground units when weather permitted during the preceding weeks, in addition to its primary assignment to the *Reichsverteidigung*. Several other Luftwaffe units that participated in *Bodenplatte* had also performed both roles in the weeks leading up to the operation, and it left JG 11 spread thinly due to its operational commitments. Only the *Stab* and II. *Gruppe* flew Bf 109G/Ks, with the rest being Fw 190A-equipped. The *Geschwaderkommodore* was Major Günther Specht, who had previously flown Bf 110 *Zerstörer*.

Although Oberstleutnant Bennemann was one of the most experienced *Jagdflieger* to take part in *Bodenplatte*, many of his pilots – including Gefreiter Alfred Michel of 16./JG 53, seen here with his head bandaged, looking forlornly at his fighter – were combat novices. Indeed, a small number were making their first sortie. Despite the widespread damage caused by JG 53 at Metz-Frescaty, the *Geschwader* as a whole lost an alarming number of aviators, including Michel, who was shot down by anti-aircraft fire in his Erla-built Bf 109G-14 Wk-Nr 462892 'Blue 2' (*Malcolm V Lowe Collection*)

Based south of Frankfurt-am-Main, the *Stab* was located at Biblis, with II. *Gruppe* at Zellhausen. These were well-established airfields that were in stark contrast to the awful conditions found at Asch.

For *Bodenplatte*, the Bf 109Gs and K-4s of II./JG 11 were the only Messerschmitts from that *Geschwader* to take part in the operation – 20 followed a Lotse Ju 88G nightfighter that took off at 0810 hrs. Prior to crossing the frontline, the Bf 109s climbed to an altitude of 350 m to cover the unit's Fw 190s, which pressed on at low-level. Allied flak rapidly accounted for several aircraft, including two of the Bf 109s.

Approaching Asch from the northeast, JG 11 prepared to attack, but at that point the unit unexpectedly flew near another Allied airfield. This was Ophoven (Y32), home to the RAF's No 125 Wing and its several Spitfire squadrons. Distracted, a number of the Fw 190s and Messerschmitts streaked over the airfield, firing at the parked Spitfires and some Dakota transports. The base's defences, initially taken by surprise, claimed several of the attackers.

At Asch, the 366th FG was already actively conducting its planned missions for that day. Thunderbolts of the unit's 390th FS were airborne, carrying single 500-lb bombs beneath each wing. Still in the airfield's vicinity, several pilots spotted gunfire at Ophoven and a large incoming formation. Dropping their bombs, the Americans waded into the JG 11 fighters. On the ground, Mustangs of the 352nd FG's 487th FS, led by Lt Col John Meyer, were preparing to take-off. With the Germans distracted by the sudden arrival of the 390th FS, the P-51 pilots rapidly took off and joined in the melee. A massive aerial battle ensued. The Mustang pilots were veterans, and made short work of several of the Messerschmitts.

Capt Henry M Stewart explained in his subsequent combat report;

'I was flying "Yellow Two" on Maj [William T] Halton's wing. Before I gave my ship the throttle on take-off, Col Meyer had one 190 spinning down in flames. I followed Maj Halton off, and he started after two 190s. They were on the deck heading east toward the frontline. I stayed at 2000 ft, giving Maj Halton cover. He got a few strikes on one 190. The ground fire got so intense I had to break. When I broke, I ran into a 109. I made a few turns with him but could not get into firing position. I followed another 109 up through the clouds at about 150 mph but could not close and almost spun out. I came back down and went around with another 109. I fired but did not observe any strikes.

'I then tagged onto a 109 heading toward our field. I closed on him and pulled the trigger, but nothing happened. My knee had shut my switches off. I got them back on and fired. I got a few strikes. We started turning over a slag pile and Capt [William T] Whisner came along and clobbered him.

'I came back toward the field again and saw two P-51s chasing a 109. The 109 broke. I cut my throttle and slid in behind him at about 100 yards and 100 ft off the deck. I fired and observed many strikes. The 109 went straight in and exploded. I pulled up to 2000 ft and started a turn. I saw another 109 on the deck heading east. I closed my throttle again and dove behind him. At 150 yards range, I opened up and got many strikes on the wing root and fuselage. The 109 went straight into the ground.

'All this time the ground fire was very intense – 0.50-cal and 20 mm. I started back toward the field and picked up another 109 on the deck, a P-51 chasing him. The P-51 broke and I dove down on the enemy aircraft, our altitude being about 100 ft. He turned, and I followed him east. I closed to 150 yards and fired, getting strikes all along the right side of the plane. Coolant came out and the 109 crashed into the ground.'

Capt Stewart claimed three victories and 1Lt Sanford Moats four.

The Thunderbolt pilots were also active, with several shooting down or damaging Fw 190s and Bf 109s. Amongst his three claims, 2Lt Melvyn R Paisley brought down at least one of the German fighters with air-to-ground rockets that he had omitted to jettison prior to the dogfight.

Despite suffering numerous losses during the fierce aerial battle with USAAF fighters, several JG 11 aircraft reached the airfield at Asch and shot up targets on the ground. A number of Mustangs and Thunderbolts were damaged, but the Germans mainly concentrated on a lone B-17. As with similar attacks at other airfields by German pilots, this was futile – the Flying Fortress was little more than a hulk that had landed at the airfield days before after suffering significant battle damage.

One of the high-profile casualties of *Bodenplatte* was Major Günther Specht, the *Geschwaderkommodore* of JG 11. An accomplished fighter pilot with 34 victories (all on the Western Front) to his name, Specht (left) is seen in this image at Wunstorf beside the tail of his Bf 109G with Professor Kurt Tank (right), who led the team that designed the Fw 190. In the centre is Hauptmann Gerhard Sommer, who was killed on 12 May 1944, shortly after this photograph was taken. Specht was killed when his Bf 109G was shot down by US fighters during JG 11's raid on Asch (*Malcolm V Lowe Collection*)

For so little gain, JG 11 suffered significant casualties. The Messerschmitts of II./JG 11 reported eight confirmed losses, and overall the *Geschwader's* toll was 24 fighters destroyed and 20 pilots killed. Amongst the latter was the *Geschwaderkommodore*, Major Günther Specht.

The 366th FG's operations report for 1 January summed up the action;

'0916 to 1048 hrs – Eight aircraft took off from the 390th FS, led by Capt Lowell B Smith. Squadron had just taken off on the mission and were forming over the field when they saw 50+ Fw 190s and Me 109s on the deck coming in from the northeast. Full bomb-load (16) and four rockets were jettisoned. Two or three of the enemy aircraft managed to make several individual passes across the field at between 50 and 500 ft altitude. Damaged by strafing was 1 P-47 Cat A, 1 P-51 Cat AC, 1 C-47 Cat A. Two men were slightly injured and one seriously.

'Enemy aircraft were taken on in a great dogfight by our planes and P-51s of the 487th Fighter Squadron, 352nd Fighter Group. Claims for the 390th Fighter Squadron are 12-2-6, and for the 487th Fighter Squadron 21-0-0. AA claims are 4-0-1. Two of our planes are Cat AC from enemy action and 1 destroyed. Pilot bailed out three miles north of base and returned. Time of attack was 0920 to 0950 hrs. Our planes returned at 1048 hrs.'

The one US loss in aerial combat was Flg Off David C Johnson of the 366th FG, who was shot down by Leutnant Walter Kohne, *Staffelkapitän* of 6./JG 11.

Later in the day, Asch was visited by 'Top Brass', including Maj Gens Hoyt S Vandenberg (commander of the Ninth Air Force) and Elwood Quesada (commander of IX Fighter Command), who passed on their congratulations to the US pilots who had defended the airfield so effectively.

SUCCESSFUL RAIDS

Eindhoven airfield (B78) was located in the comparatively small part of the Netherlands that had been liberated as a result of advances linked to Operation *Market Garden* in September 1944. A well-appointed former Luftwaffe base that had suffered little damage, it was soon home to the Typhoons of Nos 124 and 143 Wings. Each comprised four squadrons, with the latter wing being made up of RCAF units. The RAF's No 39 Wing comprising reconnaissance Spitfires and Mustangs had also moved to the airfield.

This airfield would suffer the most damage during *Bodenplatte*. Assigned to attack what had rapidly become a prime target was JG 3, led by high-scoring ace Major Heinz Bär. *Stab* and IV.(*Sturm*)/JG 3 flew the Fw 190A, while I. and III. *Gruppen* were operational with Bf 109G-14s and G-14/ASs. Representing the differing orders that were given to each participating unit in *Bodenplatte*, some of the pilots of JG 3 were instructed to turn on their radio sets upon crossing the River Rhine, but to observe radio silence, while others could only turn them on in the target area. The FuG 16 radio equipment in Bf 109s took from 60 to 90 seconds to warm up and be usable.

At 0825 hrs, the Bf 109G-14s of III./JG 3 began taking off from Bad Lippspringe near Paderborn, followed soon after by the Messerschmitts of I./JG 3 (including a number of Bf 109G-14/ASs) from Paderborn itself. Eventually, 60 fighters from the *Geschwader* – both Fw 190s and Bf 109s – crossed the Rhine and headed for Eindhoven. One was lost almost immediately, the Messerschmitt of Leutnant Hans-Ulrich Jung (*Staffelkapitän* of 10./JG 3) snagging an electricity power line. His aircraft disintegrated in a ball of flames. A 15-victories ace, Jung had previously mentioned to his *Staffel* comrades that he had had a premonition that he would not return from the mission. A second Bf 109 was lost shortly thereafter, this time to accurate US Army anti-aircraft fire. Its I. *Gruppe* pilot successfully bailed out.

One of the successful participants in the *Bodenplatte* attack was Major Heinz Bär, the *Geschwaderkommodore* of JG 3. This unit attacked Eindhoven airfield and caused considerable damage. Bär himself claimed two Typhoons shot down during the raid. He was one of the few *Geschwader* commanding officers who was able to celebrate the operation upon returning to base (*Malcolm V Lowe Collection*)

The first *Jagdflieger* to reach Eindhoven airfield was Major Bär in his Fw 190D-9, followed by other *Stab* pilots at around 0920 hrs. Just taking off were Typhoons of the RCAF's No 438 Sqn, which the Germans immediately attacked. Major Bär shot down the leading two aircraft, with both pilots being killed. Another casualty was a returning No 137 Sqn Typhoon pilot who had just landed when the Germans arrived. Messerschmitt pilot Leutnant Oskar Zimmermann, *Staffelkapitän* of 9./JG 3, apparently shot down another Typhoon over the airfield for his 30th victory.

The bomb dump of No 440 Sqn RCAF exploded during the attack, while many aircraft either at dispersal or taxiing out were destroyed. However, the airfield's anti-aircraft defences put up a considerable barrage, claiming a number of the Messerschmitts and Focke-Wulfs shot down. Sqn Ldr Gordon Wonnacott, CO of Spitfire-equipped No 414 Sqn, waded into the mixed bag of German fighters after returning early from his armed reconnaissance mission and shot down at least one of them – he claimed three destroyed prior to exhausting his ammunition.

The German attack lasted until approximately 0945 hrs, with JG 3 being joined by several aircraft from JG 6 that had supposedly been tasked to strafe Volkel airfield but had become lost when their own mission ran into problems. Finally, the Luftwaffe fighters had to turn for home before their fuel ran out. Several more were duly shot down, while others ran out of fuel or diverted to closer airfields. One of the losses amongst the departing Messerschmitts was 19-year-old Gefreiter Rudolf Wieschhoff of 4./JG 3, who was shot down and killed by anti-aircraft fire.

Overall, the JG 3 raid on Eindhoven was a success. Upon their return to Germany, the surviving pilots had a small celebration with Major Bär prior to embarking on a further mission that afternoon when they provided fighter protection for Arado Ar 234 jet bombers of KG 76.

The attack on Eindhoven left the airfield in a mess. Indeed, if all the *Bodenplatte* raids had been this successful, the Allies would certainly have felt the impact of the operation for several weeks, rather than just a matter

Although his Bf 109 was badly damaged by German anti-aircraft fire on 1 January 1945, Oberstleutnant Herbert Ihlefeld of JG 1 was able to successfully crash land and return to the unit that he led as *Geschwaderkommodore*. Starting in the late summer of 1940, he had commanded I.(J)/LG 2, the fighter component of *Jabo*-operating LG 2. This gave Ihlefeld considerable experience in the Bf 109's use as a fighter-bomber several years before the *Bodenplatte* operation. In this image, taken in 1940–41, he is posed with his Bf 109E, which bore the unit insignia of I.(J)/LG 2 on its fuselage side (*Malcolm V Lowe Collection*)

of days. Approximately 44 aircraft were destroyed, with around 60 damaged to varying degrees – these were mainly Typhoons and reconnaissance Spitfires, the German pilots in this case concentrating on the most important aircraft present, although some Dakotas and other less operationally significant types were also attacked. At least 15 Allied personnel were killed, with more than 40 wounded.

Major Bär was very pleased with his unit's performance, and later wrote;

'On New Year's Day a big operation was flown by all *Jagdverbände* over Holland and Belgium. *Jagdgeschwader* 3 attacked Eindhoven – 40-50 aircraft destroyed on the ground and 10 in the air. Two Tempests by me at 0923–0925. Aerial reconnaissance showed that of the 170 aircraft on the field, 80-100 were destroyed. Bravo!'

The operations diary of III./JG 3 enthusiastically stated, 'It would be the last big victory of the Luftwaffe, in which *Jagdgeschwader* 3, destroying 116 aircraft at Eindhoven, played a major part'. On the British side, No 143 Wing's diarist summed up the raid, and the respect shown to the German pilots, as follows;

'At 0920 hrs, two waves of mixed Fw 190s and Me 109s came onto the field at deck level, one out of the sun from East to West, the other directly down the runway, North to South. Subsequent succeeding waves of about 12 aircraft each beat up the field in a well-organised manner, the aircraft being persistent, and well-led throughout.'

JG 3's losses amongst its Bf 109s and Fw 190s were 15 shot down or lost to accidents, with nine pilots killed. Again, this was a significant blow to one of the Luftwaffe's premier combat units.

Another *Geschwader* that had needed to be re-built following major losses during June 1944 in the battle for France and the subsequent retreat was JG 1. This unit's III. *Gruppe* continued to fly the Bf 109 following its complete re-equipment, the other constituent parts of the *Geschwader* being operational on the Fw 190. As with JG 3, its *Geschwaderkommodore* was an accomplished 'old hare', Oberstleutnant Herbert Ihlefeld, who, earlier in the war, had been the commanding officer of I.(J)/LG 2. He was therefore closely acquainted with fighter-bomber operations. Leading the Messerschmitt-equipped III./JG 1 at the end of December 1944 was Hauptmann Harald Moldenhauer.

Committed to the *Reichsverteidigung*, JG 1, like other fighter units, was temporarily reassigned during December 1944 to support – when weather permitted – the German ground offensive that started on 16 December. During its Reich defence and ground support operations, JG 1 suffered significant losses. Many of those killed were young pilots who had only recently completed their training. And by then, the training curriculum was very truncated and lightweight compared to the excellent schooling that had existed in Germany pre-war and in the early stages of World War 2.

JG 1 had the responsibility of attacking three airfields in northwest Belgium during *Bodenplatte*. These were Maldegem (B65), Ursel (B67) and St Denis Westrem (B61) near Ghent. The latter was the responsibility of II./JG 1 with its Fw 190s, Ursel was delegated to IV./JG 1, again with Focke-Wulfs, while the Bf 109s of III./JG 1 would join *Stab* and I./JG 1's Fw 190s to attack Maldegem.

These airfields turned out to be ideal targets. Due to the fast-moving events of the final weeks of 1944, Maldegem and St Denis Westrem had been left behind comparatively quickly, and they were devoid of anti-aircraft defences. Maldegem was home to the Spitfires of No 135 Wing, although one of its squadrons were not present on 1 January. Ursel was empty, being mainly used as a diversion airfield and refuelling stop for units passing through.

At the time of *Bodenplatte*, III./JG 1's Messerschmitts were based at Rheine. Take-off was at approximately 0815 hrs, after which, led by a Ju 88G nightfighter, the *Gruppe* followed the Fw 190s of *Stab* and I./JG 1. Only around 12 Messerschmitts were involved. While still over occupied territory, German anti-aircraft batteries fired on the JG 1 fighters, shooting down four Fw 190s, including the aircraft of *Geschwaderkommodore* Oberstleutnant Ihlefeld – he force landed near Rotterdam. Both Lotsen Ju 88s were also destroyed.

Ironically, the flight over enemy territory proved less eventful. The combined formation arrived without incident at Bruges and turned towards Maldegem, jettisoning their drop tanks. The Fw 190s of 4./JG 1 departed en route to Ursel. Both attacks were successful. The Focke-Wulfs of *Stab* and I./JG 1 and the Messerschmitts of III./JG 1 had no problem striking at Maldegem due to the lack of organised anti-aircraft defences, although many personnel on the ground engaged the Luftwaffe aircraft with whatever small arms they could find when it was obvious that their airfield was under attack.

The raid began at around 0910 hrs. The Germans successfully shot up the airfield, destroying at least 11 Spitfires of No 485 Sqn. Some 16 aircraft were written off in total on the ground, and one Spitfire was shot down in a brief aerial encounter over the airfield. On departure, one of the Messerschmitts had to belly land due to engine failure, its pilot being taken prisoner. Two further Bf 109s were shot down by anti-aircraft fire during their return flight, with Feldwebel Wilhelm Kräuter being killed. He was one of the experienced pilots in the unit, having made seven aerial victory claims.

The attack on St Denis Westrem did not include any Messerschmitts, but it was one of the most successful raids of *Bodenplatte*, the Fw 190s of I./JG 1 causing considerable destruction. That airfield, plus Ursel and Maldegem, were subsequently photographed by camera-carrying Bf 109G-8s of 3.*Nahaufklärungsgruppe* 1, which confirmed the relative success of JG 1. Nevertheless, the unit as a whole lost 29 aircraft, with at least 16 pilots killed.

The results of the *Bodenplatte* attack were therefore mixed. In some cases considerable damage was caused, while at other locations very little was militarily accomplished. Although the whole operation achieved tactical surprise, and appears to have come as a nasty shock to the Allies, it was arguably a strategic defeat and the cost to the Luftwaffe was heavy. The losses of Bf 109 and Fw 190 airframes could be made good given time, but the death or capture of experienced airmen was irreversible. Even the loss of 'green' pilots was a blow to the already depleted *Jagdwaffe*.

American light anti-aircraft batteries had taken a considerable toll on the attackers, who also lost some of their number to their own flak units. USAAF and RAF fighters also proved to be highly capable opponents where they were able to intercept the raiders from a position of advantage.

An official listing of credited air-to-air claims by USAAF pilots was published and subsequently revised following the war. This confirmed 63 victories, plus six half-shares, for American fighter pilots on 1 January 1945. Of course, this included not just Bf 109s, but Fw 190s and their twin-engined pathfinders too. But these claims, when added to the aerial activity of 2nd TAF units, and the successes of ground defences, represent the true scale of the Luftwaffe's crippling losses during *Bodenplatte*. Without a doubt, in some cases considerable damage had been inflicted on several Allied airfields, but by that late stage in the war these losses of aircraft and infrastructure could easily be made up.

At the time of *Bodenplatte*, Generalleutnant Adolf Galland was head of the German fighter force (*General der Jagdflieger*). Suitably unhappy, he had this to say following the operation;

'The Luftwaffe received its death blow at the Ardennes offensive. In unfamiliar conditions and with insufficient training and combat experience, our numerical strength had no effect. It was decimated while in transfer, on the ground, in large air battles, especially during Christmas, and was finally destroyed. Operation *Ground Slab* [*Bodenplatte*] was the conclusion of this tragic chapter.

'In the early morning of January 1, 1945, every aircraft took off. They went into a large-scale well-prepared, low-level attack on Allied airfields in the north of France, Belgium and Holland. With this action, the enemy's air force was to be paralysed in one stroke. In good weather this large-scale action should have been made correspondingly earlier. The briefing order demanded the very greatest effort from all units. According to records, about 400 Allied aeroplanes were destroyed, but the enemy was able to replace material losses quickly. In this forced action we sacrificed our last substance. Because of terrific defensive anti-aircraft fire from the attacked airfields, from flying through barrages intended for V1 bombs, and from enemy fighters, and because of fuel shortage, we had a total loss of nearly 300 fighter pilots, including 59 leaders. Only by radically dissolving some units was it possible to retain the remainder.'

Operation *Bodenplatte* was the swansong of the Bf 109 in the air-to-ground role in the West. The practically needless loss of so many aircraft and their pilots for so little gain was a hammer blow for the Luftwaffe. Sorely needed resources for the *Reichsverteidigung* had been lost, including the death or capture of invaluable experienced pilots. The losses sustained by the Bf 109 units, together with those flying the Fw 190, were a disaster for the Germans. Although the Luftwaffe fought on often gallantly against overwhelming odds until the end of the conflict, the aerial battle was all but over before the final surrender that ended the war in Europe on 8 May 1945.

APPENDICES

COLOUR PLATES

1

Bf 109E-4/B 'Yellow 1' of Oberleutnant Otto Hintze,
Staffelkapitän of 3./ErprGr 210, Denain-Prouvy/
Calais-Marck, France, August 1940

3./ErprGr 210 was the first _Staffel_ to fly _Jabo_ Bf 109Es in combat. 'Yellow 1' was assigned to the _Staffelkapitän_, Oberleutnant Otto Hintze. The aircraft was painted in RLM 71 Dunkelgrün (dark green) and RLM 02 Grau (grey) splinter pattern camouflage on its uppersurfaces, and RLM 65 Hellblau (light blue) on the undersides. The aircraft also had a black/yellow spinner. The light blue fuselage sides of 3./ErprGr 210's Bf 109Es were made less obvious with vertical and diagonal streaks probably in RLM 02 Grau. Oberleutnant Hintze was shot down on 29 October 1940 during a _Jabo_ mission (his 52nd) to London and became a PoW.

2

Bf 109E-4/B 'Black H'+'Black Triangle' of 5.(S)/LG 2,
Calais-Marck, France, October 1940

II.(S)/LG 2 was the first _Gruppe_ to fly _Jabo_ Bf 109Es in combat, doing so alongside the pioneering 3./ErprGr 210 at Calais-Marck from early September 1940 onwards. This aircraft was unusual in carrying four 50-kg bombs on a lower fuselage ETC 50 rack. It might have borne the 5. _Staffel_ 'bear breaking umbrella' badge on its yellow cowling, although this is not confirmed. The aircraft's uppersurfaces were painted in the established 71/02 splinter pattern, plus a mottle of these colours to cover its prominent fuselage sides, with its undersides in 65. It had the standard late Battle of Britain yellow nose and rudder tactical markings, as well as a blue/white spinner.

3

Bf 109E-4/B Wk-Nr 5567 'Yellow C'+'Black Triangle' of
Feldwebel Werner Gottschalk, 6.(S)/LG 2, Calais-Marck,
France, early September 1940

The first _Jabo_ Bf 109E to fall relatively intact into British hands, Wk-Nr 5567 was force landed at RAF Hawkinge on 6 September 1940 after being damaged by anti-aircraft fire in the Chatham area. Its uppersurfaces were probably painted in the established 71/02 splinter pattern, but there is evidence from intelligence reports that the 71 Dunkelgrün was over-painted with a locally mixed greyish-green, plus a mottle of these colours to cover its prominent fuselage sides, with its undersurfaces in 65. The aircraft bore the 6.(S)/LG 2 'cat with lantern and sword' insignia on both sides of its engine cowling. Finally, it had white wingtips and rudder, with the spinner in blue/white.

4

Bf 109E-4/B Wk-Nr 5593 'White N'+'Black Triangle' of
Oberfeldwebel Josef Harmeling, 4.(S)/LG 2, Calais-Marck,
France, October 1940

Originally built by WNF as a Bf 109E-4, Wk-Nr 5593 force landed at Langenhoe, in Essex, on 29 October 1940, and its pilot, Oberfeldwebel Josef Harmeling, was taken prisoner. The aircraft was subsequently used for fund-raising and educational displays in Britain. Its uppersurfaces were painted in the established 71/02 splinter pattern, plus a mottle of these colours to cover its prominent fuselage sides, with its lower surfaces in 65. The aircraft bore the 4.(S)/LG 2 'Mickey Mouse' badge on both sides of its engine cowling. Aside from its yellow nose and rudder and blue/white spinner, there were faint traces of the aircraft's original Stammkennzeichen (factory code) on the airframe, which appeared to be DH+EJ.

5

Bf 109E-4/B Wk-Nr 3726 'Yellow M'+'Black Triangle and
Bar' of Feldwebel Erhardt Pankratz, 6.(S)/LG 2,
Calais-Marck, France, October 1940

Built by Messerschmitt at Regensburg as a Bf 109E-4/B, Wk-Nr 3726 was one of the growing number of casualties amongst the _Jabo_ aircraft of LG 2 as the Battle of Britain progressed, being brought down at Peasmarsh, in East Sussex, on 5 October. Feldwebel Erhardt Pankratz was captured wounded. The aircraft was subsequently used for fund-raising and educational displays in Britain. Its uppersurfaces were painted in the established 71/02 splinter pattern, plus a mottle of these colours to cover its prominent fuselage sides, with its undersurfaces in 65. The aircraft, which bore the 6.(S)/LG 2 insignia on both sides of its engine cowling, had a yellow nose and rudder and a blue/white spinner.

6

Bf 109E-3 'White 14' of Fähnrich Hans-Joachim Marseille,
I.(J)/LG 2, Calais-Marck, France, August 1940

The two _Gruppen_ of LG 2 often worked together, with I.(J)/LG 2's fighters escorting the _Jabos_ of I.(S)/LG 2 and sometimes flying bombing sorties of their own. Representative of I.(J)/LG 2's escorts was 'White 14' of Fähnrich Hans-Joachim Marseille, who had his somewhat inauspicious combat debut with this unit but went on to become the high-scoring 'Star of Africa' with JG 27 in the Western Desert. The aircraft's uppersurfaces were painted in the established 71/02 splinter pattern, plus a mottle of these colours to cover its prominent fuselage sides, with its lower surfaces in 65. Aside from the standard yellow nose and tail, the aircraft also had a black/white 2. _Staffel_ insignia (ex-_Legion Condor_) on its rear fuselage and possibly a white spinner.

7

Bf 109E-4/B Wk-Nr 5566 'White F'+'Black Triangle' of
Unteroffizier Georg Mörschel, 4.(S)/LG 2, Calais-Marck,
France, October 1940

Originally built as a Bf 109E-4 by WNF, Wk-Nr 5566 became locally famous by crashing onto the Spa Golf Club course in Tunbridge Wells, Kent, on 7 October and its injured pilot, Unteroffizier Georg Mörschel, being taken prisoner. Its uppersurfaces were painted in the established 71/02 splinter pattern, plus a mottle of these colours to cover its prominent fuselage sides, with its lower surfaces in 65. Again, it had a yellow nose, tail and spinner, and there were faint traces of the aircraft's original Stammkennzeichen on the airframe, which appeared to be KB+IE or +IF. The 4. _Staffel_ 'Mickey Mouse' insignia on the engine cowling was painted onto a blue circle.

8
Bf 109E-4/B Wk-Nr 4103 'Black 1' of Oberleutnant Victor Mölders, *Staffelkapitän* of 2./JG 51, Saint-Inglevert and Pihen, France, October 1940

Victor Mölders was the brother of the famous fighter pilot and tactician Werner Mölders. He force landed on 7 October at Lidham Farm near Guestling, in East Sussex, and was taken prisoner. Wk-Nr 4103 was an Erla-built Bf 109E-4/B, although it had the 'rounded top' cockpit canopy of the earlier 'Emils'. Although I./JG 51 was officially based at Saint-Inglevert, some of its Messerschmitts operated from nearby Pihen landing ground. This aircraft's uppersurfaces were painted in the established 71/02 splinter pattern, plus a relatively hard-edged mottle covering its prominent fuselage sides, with its lower surfaces in 65. The aircraft also had a yellow nose and tail and a red/white spinner.

9
Bf 109E-1/B Wk-Nr 6313 'White G'+'Black Triangle' of Unteroffizier Paul Wacker, 4.(S)/LG 2, Calais-Marck, France, November 1940

This well-known Fieseler Kassel-built Bf 109E-1/B was being flown by Unteroffizier Paul Wacker from a forward location in the Lower Normandy area on 30 November 1940 when it suffered a major engine malfunction. Wacker hastily belly landed near the historic ruin of Corfe Castle and was taken prisoner. His aircraft was subsequently repaired and sent to the US for a public tour. It was finished in the standard 71/02 splinter camouflage on its uppersurfaces and RLM 65 Hellblau on the undersides, with a very light unit-applied mottle on the fuselage sides. It is not known who the three red victory bars on the yellow rudder were achieved by.

10
Bf 109E-1B 'Black 2' (unit allocation not confirmed – possibly *Ergänzungsgruppe*/JG 51), Cazaux, France, spring 1941

This aircraft featured in a series of propaganda images, ostensibly flying in action on the Channel Front. A number of theories have been put forward as to its true identity, including being a fighter-bomber of the training unit *Ergänzungsgruppe*/JG 51. If this was indeed the case, it was based at Cazaux, in southwestern France, although that unit's 1. *Staffel* flew from Abbeville in northern France between March and May 1941. The aircraft was finished in the standard RLM 71/02 splinter camouflage on its uppersurfaces and RLM 65 Hellblau on the undersides, with a very heavy mottle on the fuselage sides seemingly mainly of RLM 71 Dunkelgrün.

11
Bf 109E-7/B 'White 1' of Oberleutnant Werner Machold, *Staffelkapitän* of 7./JG 2, Bernay, France, early 1941

During 1941 JG 2 emerged as one of the two chief fighter units on the Channel Front (with JG 26), with one of its three *Jabo Staffeln* (7./JG 2) being led by the colourful Werner Machold. He flew a number of Bf 109s, including this one while he was stationed at Bernay that featured his impressive tally of aerial victories on its rudder. Machold was primarily a fighter pilot, and not wholeheartedly a *Jabo* exponent. The aircraft was finished in the standard 71/02 splinter camouflage on its uppersurfaces and RLM 65 Hellblau underneath, with a very light mottle on the fuselage sides. Aside from its yellow rudder and nose, the fighter had a black spinner, JG 2's 'Richthofen' insignia below the windscreen and 7. *Staffel's*

emblem on the nose. Bf 109E-7s set-up for *Jabo* sorties were sometimes designated without the '/B' prefix.

12
Bf 109E-1/B Wk-Nr 6327 'Brown 7' of Feldwebel Ernst Schultz, 9./JG 27, Guines, France, September 1940

Built by Fieseler at Kassel, this was one of the comparatively few Bf 109E-1/Bs to participate in the Battle of Britain. It was force landed at Sellindge, Kent, on 18 September 1940 by Feldwebel Ernst Schultze during one of the first *Jabo* raids undertaken by a unit other than 3./ErprGr 210 and LG 2. Schultze was shot through the chest while trying to escape from the downed Bf 109 and he died of his wounds on 26 September. The aircraft's uppersurfaces were painted in the established 71/02 splinter pattern, plus a mottle of these colours to cover its prominent fuselage sides, with its lower surfaces in 65. It had a yellow rudder and nose and a yellow/brown spinner. The 'Brown 7' was painted in a somewhat unusual position that was almost unique to JG 27.

13
Bf 109E-4/B Wk-Nr 1106 'Yellow 1' of Oberleutnant Walter Rupp, *Staffelkapitän* of 3./JG 53, Le Touquet, France, October 1940

Beginning life as an Erla-built Bf 109E-3, Rupp's aircraft was brought up to roughly E-4/B standard. He force landed it at RAF Manston on 17 October 1940, and the fighter-bomber was subsequently used for fund-raising and educational displays in Britain. Similar to a number of other Bf 109Es from JG 53, this *Jabo* featured non-standard camouflage. The established scheme of RLM 71/02 splinter camouflage on its uppersurfaces and RLM 65 Hellblau underneath was transformed on the fuselage with additional camouflage added at unit level that apparently featured irregular areas of RLM 71 Dunkelgrün and also RLM 70 Schwarzgrün. It had a standard yellow spinner, nose and rudder. The infamous JG 53 red band was partly obscured presumably during a re-paint of the yellow cowling panels.

14
Bf 109E-4/B Wk-Nr 5801 'Black 7' of Oberleutnant Walter Fiel, 8./JG 53, Le Touquet, France, early October 1940

A WNF-built *Jabo*, Wk-Nr 5801 force landed at Addlested Farm in East Peckham, Kent, on 2 October 1940 after it was attacked by 16+ Spitfires, Oberleutnant Fiel being taken prisoner. It was finished in the standard 71/02 splinter camouflage on its uppersurfaces and RLM 65 Hellblau on the undersides, with random mottle on the fuselage sides. Aside from its yellow tactical markings and red/white spinner, the aircraft also featured JG 53's red band around its nose.

15
Bf 109F-4/B Wk-Nr 7629 'Blue 1'+'Chevron and Bar' of Oberleutnant Frank Liesendahl, *Staffelkapitän* of 10.(*Jabo*)/ JG 2, Beaumont-le-Roger, France, May–June 1942

Liesendahl's personal WNF-built Bf 109F-4/B was painted in the mid-war greys of RLM 74 and 75 on its uppersurfaces and RLM 76 blue-grey on the undersides. It had a yellow rudder, onto which a growing scoreboard of merchant ships sunk or attacked was added. The *Staffel* insignia of a dark red fox with a broken ship in its mouth was applied on the engine cowling. Liesendahl was shot down and killed on 17 July 1942 while participating in one of the unit's first fighter-bomber anti-shipping attacks with the new Fw 190A *Jabo*.

16

Bf 109F-4/B 'Blue 7'+'Chevron and Bar' of 10.(*Jabo*)/JG 2, Beaumont-le-Roger, France, May 1942

With its rudder featuring a scoreboard of anti-shipping claims in a similar style to 'Blue 1' seen in the previous profile, this aircraft is something of a mystery. Either several aircraft in the squadron had rudder markings that showcased the achievements of the entire *Staffel*, or this Bf 109F-4/B later became 'Blue 1'. The Messerschmitt fighter-bombers of Liesendahl's 10.(*Jabo*)/JG 2 were very smartly finished in the mid-war greys of RLM 74 and 75 on their uppersurfaces and RLM 76 blue-grey on their undersides.

17

Bf 109F-4/B Wk-Nr 7232 'White 11' of Unteroffizier Oswald Fischer, 10.(*Jabo*)/JG 26, Caen-Carpiquet, France, June 1942

One of the most famous Bf 109F examples was Unteroffizier Fischer's 'White 11', which he force landed at Beachy Head after taking hits while attacking shipping off Newhaven. With the white falling bomb symbol of 10.(*Jabo*)/JG 26 on its rear fuselage, 'White 2' was typical of the Bf 109F-4/B *Jabos* of this unit, with its mid-war greys camouflage of 74/75 on its uppersurfaces and 76 on the undersides. The aircraft was subsequently repaired and flew again with the RAF as NN644.

18

Bf 109F-4/B Wk-Nr 7232 NN644 (formerly 'White 11') of No 1426 (Enemy Aircraft) Flight, RAF Collyweston, England, late 1943

Fischer's Bf 109F-4/B Wk-Nr 7232 had a second life with the RAF after it was repaired, being flown in Britain by No 1426 (Enemy Aircraft) Flight. Painted in RAF colours of Dark Green and Ocean Grey uppersurfaces and yellow undersides, the aircraft had roundels and a fin flash applied in the usual locations for day fighters and the British military serial NN644 added to the fighter-bomber's rear fuselage. The aircraft was eventually scrapped post-war.

19

Bf 109F-4/B Wk-Nr 8532 'White 2' of Feldwebel Otto Görtz, 10.(*Jabo*)/JG 26, Caen-Carpiquet, France, June 1942

Also displaying 10.(*Jabo*)/JG 26's distinctive insignia on its rear fuselage, 'White 2' was typical of the Bf 109F-4/B *Jabos* of this unit, with its mid-war greys camouflage of 74/75 on its uppersurfaces and 76 on the undersides. The aircraft was shot down into the sea by anti-aircraft fire while on an evening raid against Bournemouth, then in Hampshire, on 6 June 1942. Feldwebel Görtz was killed.

20

Bf 109F-4/B Wk-Nr 13005 'Blue 12'+'Chevron and Bar' of Obergefreiter Franz Langhammer, 10.(*Jabo*)/JG 2, Beaumont-le-Roger, France, April 1942

As previously noted, the Bf 109F-4/B fighter-bombers of Frank Liesendahl's 10.(*Jabo*)/JG 2 were very smartly finished in the mid-war greys of 74 and 75 on their uppersurfaces and 76 blue-grey on lower surfaces. This aircraft did not carry the 'ships' scoreboard' on its rudder, further deepening the mystery of this marking that apparently appeared on some but not all of the unit's *Jabos*. Langhammer was shot down into the sea in this aircraft on 21 April 1942 during a *Jabo* attack on Wakeham, on the Isle of Portland in Dorset – he was the first loss to be suffered by 10.(*Jabo*)/JG 2.

21

Bf 109G-14 Wk-Nr 781183 'Blue 3' of Unteroffizier Werner Zetzschke, 4./JG 4, Darmstadt-Griesheim, Germany, 1 January 1945

This aircraft was manufactured by Messerschmitt at Regensburg. Late war colour schemes of these aircraft are contentious, and there is a train of thought that the Messerschmitt-built machines were painted in the mid-war greys of 74/75/76 (as depicted here), but equally that the 74 was progressively superseded by RLM 83 (a mid-green) and the 75 was also eventually replaced, by RLM 81 (a brownish-green that existed in several different incarnations). The vertical tail, made by a sub-contractor, is believed to have had an RLM 75 grey base with RLM 62 green blotches and RLM 76 blue-grey streaks. The aircraft's spinner was black/white, and JG 4's black/white/black *Reichsverteidigung* bands adorned the rear fuselage. The *Jagdgeschwader*'s insignia was also carried on the nose of the fighter. Zetzschke was killed when this aircraft crashed in the Dutch town of Sittard during *Bodenplatte*.

22

Bf 109G-14/AS Wk-Nr 784986 'Yellow 19' of Oberfeldwebel Paul Schwerdtfeger, 11./JG 6, Bissel, Germany, 1 January 1945

Manufactured by Messerschmitt at Regensburg, there is similarly controversy over the colouring of the Bf 109G-14/AS machines, with ideas ranging from 74/75/76 to 82/75/76 and 81/82/76. Taking part in the failed attack on Volkel airfield, this aircraft was hit by ground fire and crashed near Groesbeek, in the Netherlands, killing Oberfeldwebel Schwerdtfeger. Bearing the red/white/red *Reichsverteidigung* rear fuselage bands of JG 6, the fighter had a black/white spinner and prominent streaks of RLM 76 blue-grey on the vertical tail as seen on Wk-Nr 781183 in the previous profile.

23

Bf 109G-14 Wk-Nr 462892 'Blue 2' of Gefreiter Alfred Michel, 16./JG 53, Stuttgart-Echterdingen, Germany, 1 January 1945

One of the many casualties of the *Bodenplatte* raid, this Erla-built Bf 109G-14 appeared to have had several changes of identity judging by the heavy over-painting of numbers on its fuselage sides. Early Erla-built Bf 109G-14s were finished in the 74/75/76 mid-war greys, but a switch was made during production to RLM 81/82, as depicted here, to replace previous uppersurface colours. It featured the black rear fuselage band of JG 53 in the *Reichsverteidigung* fighter arm, and had a black/white spinner. The inexperienced Michel survived being brought down by anti-aircraft fire.

24

Bf 109G-14/U4 Wk-Nr 512335 'Black 5' of Gefreiter Othmar Heberling, 2./JG 77, Dortmund, Germany, 1 January 1945

A WNF-manufactured Bf 109G-14, 'Black 5' participated in the attack against Antwerp-Duerne that was largely unsuccessful during the *Bodenplatte* raid, even though it was a prime target. The aircraft carried the red 'Ace of Hearts' unit insignia on its cowling and a Zylinderhut (top hat) on the rear fuselage. The latter was a marking previously used by the *Legion Condor* and, later, I.(J)/LG 2. The aircraft was probably finished in 74/75/76, although WNF, like Erla, also changed to 81/82 uppersurface colours during production of the Bf 109G-14, replacing the 74/75 greys. The spinner was black/white.

SELECTED SOURCES

Bekker, Cajus, *The Luftwaffe War Diaries – The German Air Force in World War II*, Ballantine Books, 1975

Forsyth, Robert, et. al., *Schlachtflieger – Luftwaffe Ground-attack Units 1937–1945*, Midland Publishing, 2007

Galland, Adolf, *The First and the Last*, Methuen, 1955

Goss, Chris, with Cornwell, Peter, and Rauchbach, Bernd, *Luftwaffe Fighter-Bombers over Britain – The Tip and Run Campaign 1942–1943*, Crécy Publishing, 2013

Holmes, Tony, *Osprey Aircraft of the Aces 18 – Hurricane Aces 1939-40,* Osprey Publishing, 1998

Laureau, Patrick, *Condor – The Luftwaffe in Spain 1936–1939*, Hikoki Publications, 2000

Manhro, John, and Pütz, Ron, *Bodenplatte: The Luftwaffe's Last Hope – The Attack on Allied Airfields New Year's Day 1945*, Hikoki Publications, 2004

Mombeek, Eric, *Luftwaffe Colours Volume One Section 2 – Jagdwaffe: The Spanish Civil War*, Classic Publications, 1999

Mombeek, Eric, *Luftwaffe Colours Volume One Section 3 – Jagdwaffe: Blitzkrieg and Sitzkrieg, Poland and France 1939–1940*, Classic Publications, 1999

Mombeek, Eric, *Luftwaffe Colours Volume One Section 4 – Jagdwaffe: Attack in the West May 1940*, Classic Publications, 2000

Mombeek, Eric, *Luftwaffe Colours Volume Two Section 1 – Jagdwaffe: Battle of Britain Phase One July–August 1940*, Classic Publications, 2001

Mombeek, Eric, *Luftwaffe Colours Volume Two Section 2 – Jagdwaffe: Battle of Britain Phase Two August–September 1940*, Classic Publications, 2001

Olynyk, Frank, *Stars and Bars – A Tribute to the American Fighter Ace 1920–1973*, Grub Street, 1995

Parker, Nigel, *Luftwaffe Crash Archive Volumes 3, 4, 5, 6 and 9*, Red Kite, 2013–16

Price, Alfred, *Luftwaffe Handbook 1939–1945*, Ian Allan, 1977

Shores, Christopher, and Thomas, Chris, *2nd Tactical Air Force Volume Two – Breakout to Bodenplatte July 1944 to January 1945*, Classic Publications, 2005

Stedman, Robert, *Osprey Warrior 122 – Jagdflieger: Luftwaffe Fighter Pilot 1939–45*, Osprey Publishing, 2008

Ullmann, Michael, *Luftwaffe Colours 1935–1945*, Hikoki Publications, 2002

Weal, John, *Osprey Aircraft of the Aces 11 – Bf 109D/E Aces 1939-41*, Osprey Publishing, 1996

Weal, John, *Osprey Aircraft of the Aces 68 – Bf 109 Defence of the Reich Aces*, Osprey Publishing, 2006

Weal, John, *Osprey Aviation Elite Units 1 – Jagdgeschwader 2 'Richthofen'*, Osprey Publishing, 2000

Weal, John, *Osprey Aviation Elite Units 12 – Jagdgeschwader 27 'Afrika'*, Osprey Publishing, 2003

Weal, John, *Osprey Aviation Elite Units 13 – Luftwaffe Schlachtgruppen*, Osprey Publishing, 2003

Weal, John, *Osprey Aviation Elite Units 22 – Jagdgeschwader 51 'Mölders'*, Osprey Publishing, 2006

Weal, John, *Osprey Aviation Elite Units 25 – Jagdgeschwader 53 'Pik As'*, Osprey Publishing, 2007

Albert F Simpson Historical Research Center, *USAF Credits for the Destruction of Enemy Aircraft, World War II: USAF Historical Study No. 85*, USAF Air University, Maxwell Air Force Base, Alabama, 1978

Transcripts and notes from interviews with former Luftwaffe personnel, including interview text from the John Batchelor archive

INDEX